DESIGN AND MAKE
YOUR OWN
DOLL'S HOUSE FURNITURE

~

DESIGN AND MAKE
YOUR OWN
DOLL'S HOUSE FURNITURE

~

HEADLEY HOLGATE AND PAMELA RUDDOCK

THE
APPLE
PRESS

A QUINTET BOOK

Published by The Apple Press
6 Blundell Street
London N7 9BH

ISBN 1-85076-469-7

This book was designed and produced by
Quintet Publishing Limited
6 Blundell Street
London N7 9BH

Creative Director: Richard Dewing
Designer: Ian Hunt
Illustrator: Andy Watkins
Project Editor: Katie Preston
Editor: Lydia Darbyshire
Photographer: Chas Wilder

Typeset in Great Britain by
Central Southern Typesetters, Eastbourne
Manufactured in Singapore by Colour Trend
Printed in Singapore by
Star Standard Industries (Pte) Ltd

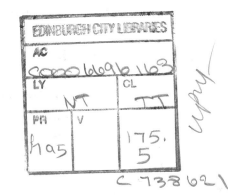

CONTENTS

~

Introduction 6

THE KITCHEN

~

THE BEDROOM

~

THE DINING ROOM

~

THE LIVING ROOM

~

Introduction

The projects in this book are set out room by room to give you ideas to fill your entire doll's house. Each room has three to four major pieces of furniture and also some smaller accessories. The larger pieces are made entirely from wood and the smaller projects use a range of materials (a full list is given at the beginning of each mini-project).

All the projects have figure diagrams showing the exact measurements of the components of the pieces. These are not drawn full size, but can be enlarged easily.

TOOLS AND EQUIPMENT

The main pieces of wooden furniture can be made with power or hand tools, depending on what equipment you already have, and which you are most familiar with; the step-by-step photographs show the furniture being constructed with the range of power tools listed below. The other pieces of equipment and accessories you will need are also listed.

Accuracy is of prime importance when working on such a small scale. It is therefore important that you constantly check the way the pieces are fitting together: whether all the legs sit squarely to the floor, for example. If you are using power tools, remember to check them regularly: for example, check that all saws are vertical to the machine table; check that your mitre gauge is set at 90°.

You will find it useful to make a basic assembly jig, which will help to check that corners are square; you can easily make one from three pieces of 12mm (½in) plywood glued at right angles to each other (see figure drawing).

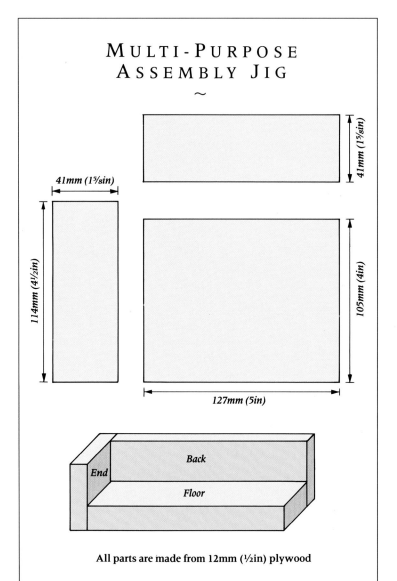

MULTI-PURPOSE
ASSEMBLY JIG
~

41mm (1⅝in)

41mm (1⅝in)

114mm (4½in)

105mm (4in)

127mm (5in)

Back

End

Floor

All parts are made from 12mm (½in) plywood

HAND TOOLS
~

Carpenter's hammer
Tack hammer
Chisels, Gouges
Screwdrivers, Craft knife
Punch, Hand fretsaw
Handsaws, Pliers
Tweezers, Vice

POWER TOOLS
~

Bandsaw with fence and circle cutting pin, Mitre gauge
Power drill and stand with bits
Router and moulding bits
Circular saw, Belt sander
Small lathe and tools
Fretsaw
Drum sanders

ACCESSORIES
~

Set square, Steel rule
Bulldog clips, Elastic bands
G-clamps, Panel pins
Wooden cocktail sticks
Metal tape measure
Brass knobs, Brass feet
Garnet papers

MATERIALS AND TECHNIQUES

Timber

There are specialist shops which deal in equipment for making doll's house furniture, and they will sell small amounts of wood to the thicknesses required for this scale of working. Alternatively, you may find a timber merchant, joiner or carpenter who will supply you with cut sections. You will probably find it most useful to obtain pieces about 300 × 125mm (12 × 5in) long and wide and from 3mm to 16mm (⅛ to ⅝in) thick. This will give you a choice of sizes that can be sliced to the required size.

The projects use three types of wood, although you may find alternatives. They are:

MAHOGANY Danta – a mahogany-type timber from the Ivory Coast – has been used in some projects. It has a very small and pleasing grain, but has the disadvantage of moving and twisting.

PINE Always make sure you use good-quality pine, since poor-quality pine is difficult to saw and sand.

PLYWOOD Available in a range of thicknesses, from 1.5mm (1/16in) upwards. It is often used for the backs of pieces, since this side is not often seen. Plywood does not twist as wood strips are apt to. It is often used as a backing to veneer.

Glues

Always suit the glue to the job in hand.

WOOD GLUE This is the type used most often in the main projects. It is used for gluing wood to wood.

TWO-PART EPOXY RESIN This is used for gluing wood to metal. Use the slow-drying variety, which takes approximately 16 hours to dry. This glue consists of an adhesive and a hardener mixed together; follow the manufacturer's instructions carefully.

MULTI-PURPOSE ADHESIVE This clear or white household glue is used for gluing fabric, such as chair seats and other upholstery.

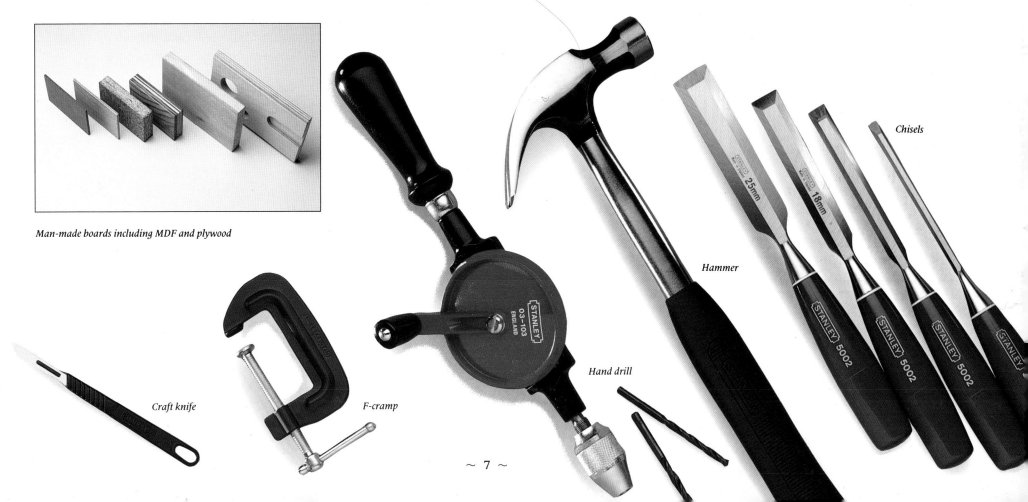

Man-made boards including MDF and plywood

Craft knife

F-cramp

Hand drill

Hammer

Chisels

Finishing

All the instructions indicate when and how each piece should be finished – that is, when it should be sanded, stained, polished and waxed. Where a piece has a large and prominent surface, for example the top, you will have to take a lot of care to finish it properly, applying up to eight coats of polish and leaving to dry overnight.

SANDING It is better to do as much finishing as possible to individual parts before you undertake any assembly. Garnet papers are best for cutting and smoothing work. They are graded by grit numbers, the lower numbers being coarse, the higher numbers finer. Grade 40 or 60 paper

---

FINISHING EQUIPMENT

~

Garnet papers in a range of grits from 40 to 360
Dusters, Cotton cloths, Stains, Sealer
Wire wool, grade 0000
Wax (containing beeswax)
Methylated spirits, Cotton wool, Polish
Burnishing cream

Wire wool grade 0000

---

should be used first for rough-sawn surfaces. Use 100 or 120 grit for a planed or smoother surface, then use 180 or 200 grit. Next use 240 grit, before giving the wood a final rubbing down with 320 or 360 grit. This programme is for perfectionists, and it can be modified if you wish. You can make or purchase a sanding block around which the paper is wrapped to produce a more even surface. All the dust that is generated must be removed with a cloth or brush before you begin to apply stain or to use any other finishing technique.

STAINING Apply the stain with a rag, although a small brush is useful for getting into difficult corners. Work with the grain. When the work is covered, wipe off any surplus stain with a clean cloth, before leaving the piece to dry overnight. When it is completely dry the surface may appear to be slightly rough. This will be the result of dust or the stain raising the grain. Use a very fine grit paper to smooth the surface.

TOP TO BOTTOM: fine garnet paper, coarse garnet paper, coarse aluminium oxide paper

---

SEALING Sealer is applied for several reasons: it affords some protection to the wood; it slightly hardens the surface; and it prevents the stain from bleeding. You should apply the sealer with a brush or a cotton cloth. The first stroke is made across the grain to lodge the talc filler that is in the sealer into the grain lines. Work quickly because sealer becomes tacky in a very short time. Leave it to dry for 24 hours. If the sealer is absorbed by the wood, apply a second or even a third coat. Rub down with a fine-grade sandpaper between coats.

WAXING A paste in which beeswax is the main ingredient is the most suitable. The first application of the wax should be made with a small piece of the finest grade, 0000, steel wool. Use plenty of wax for this first application and work with the grain. Wipe off any surplus or strands of steel wool with a clean cloth. Leave to harden overnight. The surface can then be polished with a clean, soft duster.

SAFETY

~

Almost all finishing materials and adhesives are toxic. Take great care when you are using or handling them. Work in a well-ventilated room and avoid inhaling either fumes or dust. Store all materials safely and make sure that all waste is disposed of in the proper way. Observe fire precautions at all times, and never smoke in your workshop. Wear protective clothing in case you spill anything. Never store finishers in old food containers and keep them all out of the reach of children.

FRENCH POLISHING
~

You will need
- 1 piece of thin cotton rag, approximately 51 × 51mm (2 × 2in)
- Methylated spirits
- Cotton wool
- Polish

FORMING THE PAD

1. Soak the cotton rag with methylated spirits and squeeze out any surplus.

2. Place the rag on a flat surface, add a ball of cotton wool and pour on the polish.

3. Turn up the edges of the rag to form a pad.

2

4

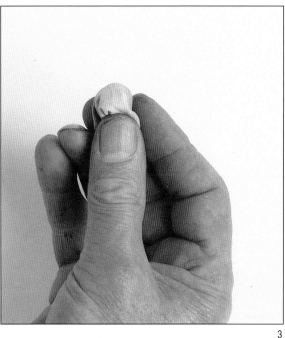

1

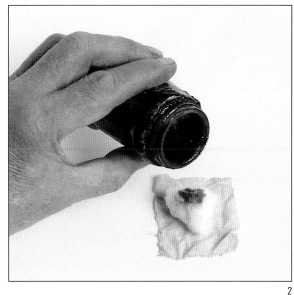

3

4. Tap the completed pad against a clean surface or the palm of your other hand until the polish appears through the rag. It is very easy to overload a pad with polish. If you do, squeeze out the pad to remove the excess. If the pad is too dry, add more polish. With practice you will learn to put in the correct amount.

POLISHING Stroke the pad along the grain. If you are polishing one piece at a time, allow each coat to dry for three to five minutes before you apply the next. For larger, more visible surfaces apply up to eight coats; five or six coats should be sufficient for smaller surfaces. Allow to dry overnight.

BURNISHING Use a burnishing cream on a piece of rag for the final finish. Apply as for French polish. When it is dry, rub with a soft duster.

Pinning blanks

Between six and eight blanks can be pinned together depending on their thickness and the length of the drill bit. This will produce several identical shapes from just one cutting process.

ICCU The position of the pins will depend on the piece being made – under the seat between the legs for chairs, for example. The length of the pin should be such that, when it is driven into the block, the heads are flush with the top of the block, but the pointed ends protrude by 1–2mm (approximately $\frac{1}{16}$in) at the bottom.

Place the assembly jig on the drill table. Adjust the depth of drilling to 1–2mm ($\frac{1}{16}$in) from the jig floor. This will fasten the bottom blank more firmly and stop it from falling off. Place the blanks on the jig and drill both pin holes. Hold the blanks together with your fingers and drive the pins into the holes with a heavy hammer. Sand the pin tips so that they are flush.

Drill a hole through the blanks for the pin.

Drive the pin into the block until the head is flush with the top.

GLOSSARY OF TERMS

CARCASS The basic framework of a piece.

CHAMFER A narrow, flat surface angled at 45°, planed or carved on the edge of a section.

COLUMN The decorative part of the leg, attached to the underside of the table, that is moulded and shaped.

COVER SLIP A small, thin strip of wood that covers the rough front edge of a slice of wood.

CROSS-CUT Cutting across the grain.

GROOVE A long, narrow channel cut into the wood. Grooves act mainly as shelf bearers.

JIG A guide to accuracy used in assembly to ensure the correct angles are held while the glue sets, and also as a guide when sawing.

LATERAL The pieces of the *carcass* that fit horizontally.

LEG HOLDER The second component of a complex leg construction. It is a small, round section of wood with three slits cut at 120° to each other, into which the legs fit.

LIPPED DRAWER A drawer which has an additional front piece which overlaps the drawer front beneath by approximately 1.5mm ($\frac{1}{16}$in).

MIDDLE UPRIGHT The pieces of the *carcass* that fit vertically.

MITRE A corner joint formed between two pieces of material, for example wood, by cutting the ends at equal angles, for example two angles of 45° joining to make a right angle of 90°.

REBATE A step cut along the edge of a piece of wood, into which another piece of wood fits – often used to hold the back of a piece.

SPLAT A piece of wood that forms the horizontal central part of a chair back. The splat may be plain or a decorative feature.

STOP A small square of wood which fits into a groove to prevent a shelf, for example, from moving in the groove.

UPSTANDS The decorative edging on the top of the desk that consists of three strips of wood fitted into grooves in the top.

VENEER A thin layer of wood with a decorative or fine finish that is bonded to the surface of a less expensive material, for example plywood.

The Kitchen

~

Kitchen Table

~

This lovely pine table is a perfect centrepiece in any kitchen. Choose a good piece of pine with a pretty grain for the top, since this element will be the most visible. The construction is relatively simple, but the detailing – such as the mitred edging and the shaped legs – makes the piece very special.

~

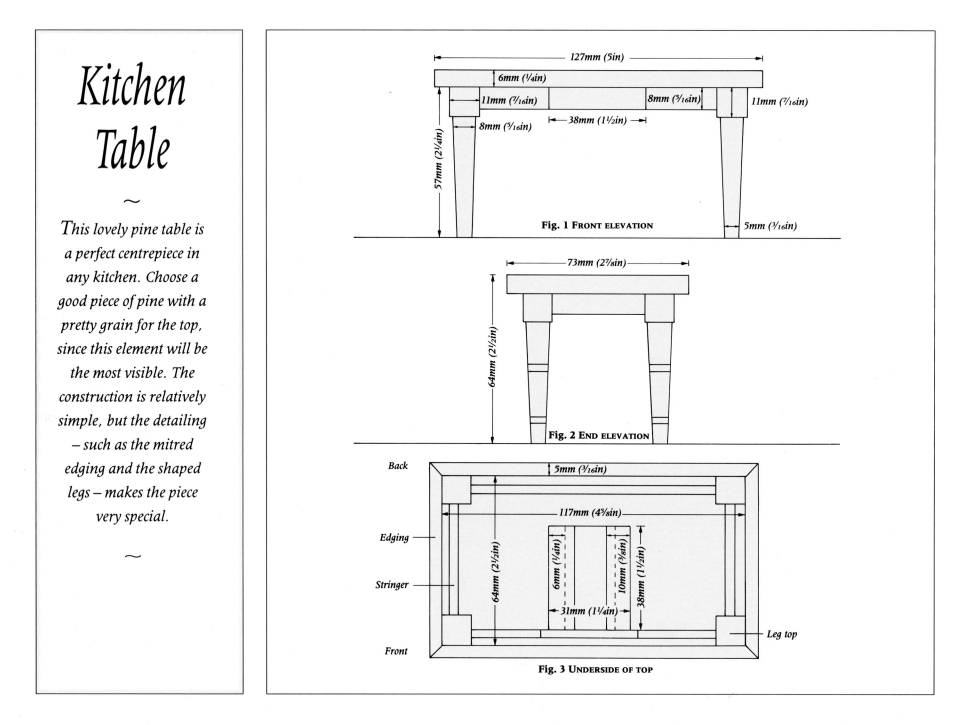

127mm (5in)

6mm (¼in)

11mm (⁷⁄₁₆in)   8mm (⁵⁄₁₆in)   11mm (⁷⁄₁₆in)

8mm (⁵⁄₁₆in)   38mm (1½in)

57mm (2¼in)

5mm (³⁄₁₆in)

Fig. 1 FRONT ELEVATION

73mm (2⅞in)

64mm (2½in)

Fig. 2 END ELEVATION

Back

5mm (³⁄₁₆in)

117mm (4⅝in)

Edging

Stringer

64mm (2½in)

6mm (¼in)   10mm (³⁄₈in)   38mm (1½in)

31mm (1¼in)

Leg top

Front

Fig. 3 UNDERSIDE OF TOP

MAKING THE TOP

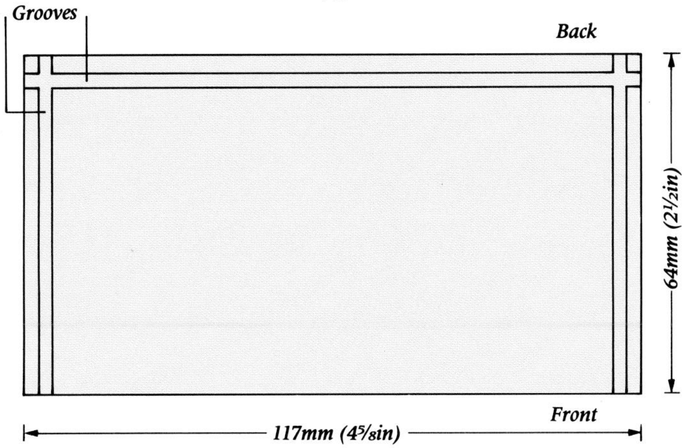

~

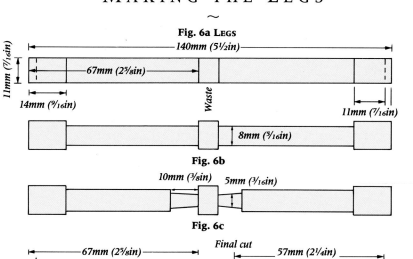

Fig. 4 **UNDERSIDE OF TOP TO SHOW GROOVES**

Grooves

Back

Front

64mm (2½in)

117mm (4⅝in)

1. Cut a piece of pine for the table top 117 × 64 × 6 mm (4⅝ × 2½ × ¼ in). Run grooves for the back and end stringers 3 mm (⅛ in) wide and deep and 3 mm (⅛ in) from the edges.

2. For the edging, cut a section 51 × 5 × 137 mm (2 × ³⁄₁₆ × 5⅜ in). You will need a 137 mm (5⅜in) strip for the back and two end strips 83 mm (3¼ in) long. Mitre the ends of the edging strips to 45°, testing for fit against the table top. Glue the strips to the table top. Hand sand or belt sand the table surface.

Approximately 51mm (2in)

5mm (³⁄₁₆in)

137mm (5⅜in)

Fig. 5 **SECTION FOR EDGING**

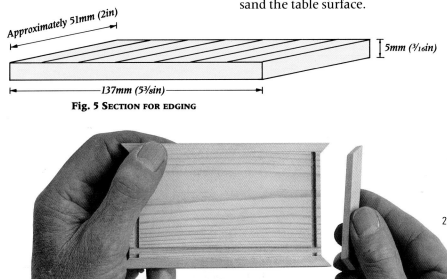

MAKING THE LEGS

~

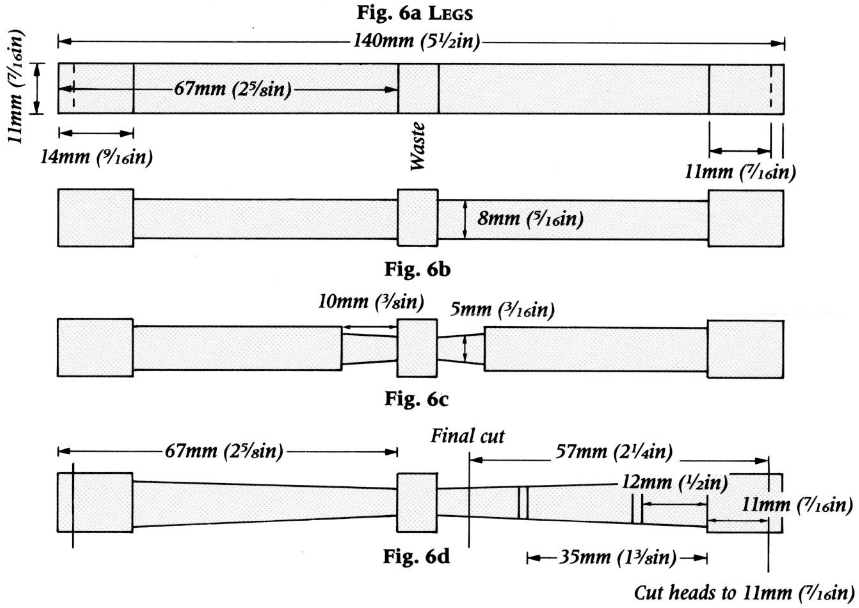

Fig. 6a **LEGS**

140mm (5½in)

11mm (⁷⁄₁₆in)

67mm (2⅝in)

14mm (⁹⁄₁₆in)

Waste

11mm (⁷⁄₁₆in)

8mm (⁵⁄₁₆in)

Fig. 6b

10mm (³⁄₈in)   5mm (³⁄₁₆in)

Fig. 6c

Final cut

67mm (2⅝in)

57mm (2¼in)

12mm (½in)

11mm (⁷⁄₁₆in)

Fig. 6d   35mm (1⅜in)

Cut heads to 11mm (⁷⁄₁₆in)

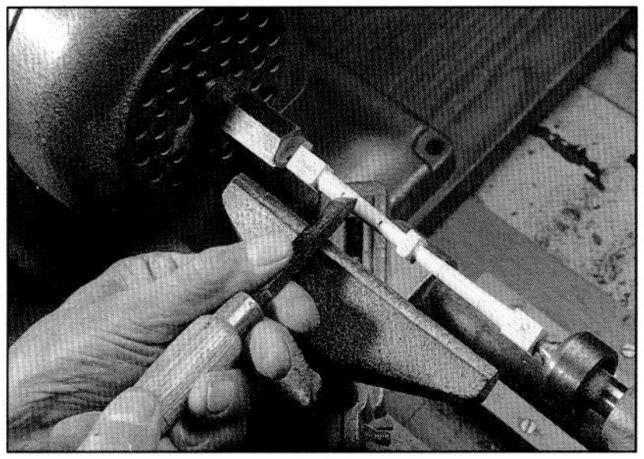

3. Cut two square blanks for the legs. Each blank will make two legs – the centre of the blank is the foot. Shape the blank in the sequence illustrated: turn the blank until it is 8 mm (⁵⁄₁₆ in) in diameter; turn the foot until it is 5 mm (³⁄₁₆ in), cut it at a slight taper to match with the total taper; taper the legs and sand; run the rings. Sand the square heads. Dust, wax and polish.

4. Cut the leg heads to 11 mm (⁷⁄₁₆ in), making sure that all the leg heads are exactly the same height. Make the final cut to the legs to give a total length of 57 mm (2¼ in). Sand the end of the legs and heads with fine sandpaper.

5. For the back and end stringers, cut a piece of pine 11 × 108 × 3 mm ($^7/_{16}$ × 4$^1/_4$ × $^1/_8$ in) long. Check the fit across the width of the groove. Sand, dust and wax one side of all the strips. Measure each piece against the underside of the table, with the legs in place, and then cut to fit.

6. For the front stringer run a section 10 mm × 108 mm ($^3/_8$ × 4$^1/_4$ in). The front stringer, which is initially glued to the drawer front, will have two cuts made in it to free the drawer front, and it needs to be cut slightly longer than the back stringer to compensate for this. Make two cuts to the drawer front strip and check that the three joined pieces exactly match the back stringer.

7. Choose the two best legs for the front of the table. Apply glue to one back leg and to the table top and glue in place. Put glue into the back groove and insert the stringer, checking for upright. Glue the second back leg. Glue the end stringers and front legs in the same way.

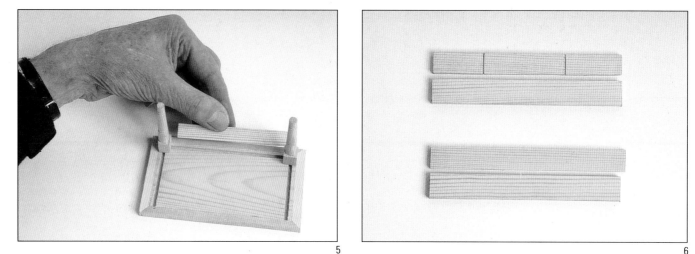

5

6

7

8. Cut the drawer bottom 1.5 mm (¹/₁₆ in) thick. Cut a section (see Fig. 5 as for edging) and slice strips 6 × 38 mm (¼ × 1½ in) for the drawer sides. Glue the sides to the bottom and leave to dry. Glue the front stringer to the drawer front matching the centre of the drawer to a centre mark on the stringer.

Fig. 7 THE DRAWER

31mm (1¼in)

38mm (1½in)

Bottom plan

Back

6mm (¼in)

Sides

Approximately 89mm (3½in)

Centres of stringer
and drawer carcasses

16mm (⅝in)

Runner foundation

Runner

Drawer back

Drawer carcass side

Drawer bottom

45mm (1¾in)

8

9. Separate the drawer front from the rest of the stringer. The ends should protrude 3 mm (⅛ in) from the drawer sides. Cut and fit the drawer back (Fig. 7).

9

10

114mm (4½in)

89mm (3½in)

Fig. 8 ASSEMBLY JIG

10. Make the assembly jig (see Fig. 8). Position the drawer and front stringer and push the assembly jig against pieces. Make sure that the gaps between the ends of the drawer front and the stringers are the same. Cut a section for the drawer runner foundations (as Fig. 5) but add the height of the drawer bottom to the thickness of the piece. Slice two foundation strips 6 mm (¼ in) wide. Cut the strips 38 mm (1½ in) long. Glue the foundations to the drawer. When the glue is dry, glue the side parts of the front stringer to the table top.

11. Make the drawer runners by cutting two strips 10 × 1.5 × 38 mm (⅝ × ⅟16 × 1½ in). Glue the strips to the runner foundations. Make sure the glue does not jam the drawer. Drill a hole in the drawer front for a brass knob 3 mm (⅛ in) in diameter.

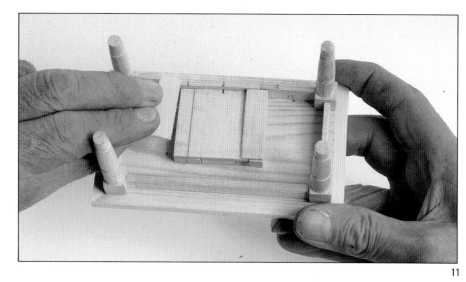

11

Alternative Method

~

You can make this table without the grooves. Proceed in the same way, but make the stringers 8 mm (⅝ in) high. Instead of placing the back and end stringers in grooves, they will have to be assembled using the jig as described for the front stringers and drawer front. Make a smaller jig in the same way for the end stringers, or assemble them by eye.

Kitchen Bench

~

A lovely accompaniment to the kitchen table (page 12), this bench, also made in pine, uses some of the same design features, such as the mitred edging. The legs are made by constructing an A-frame and slicing cross-sections from the frame. This means the leg pieces are exactly the same height and shape, and it also makes it easier to create more than one bench at a time.

~

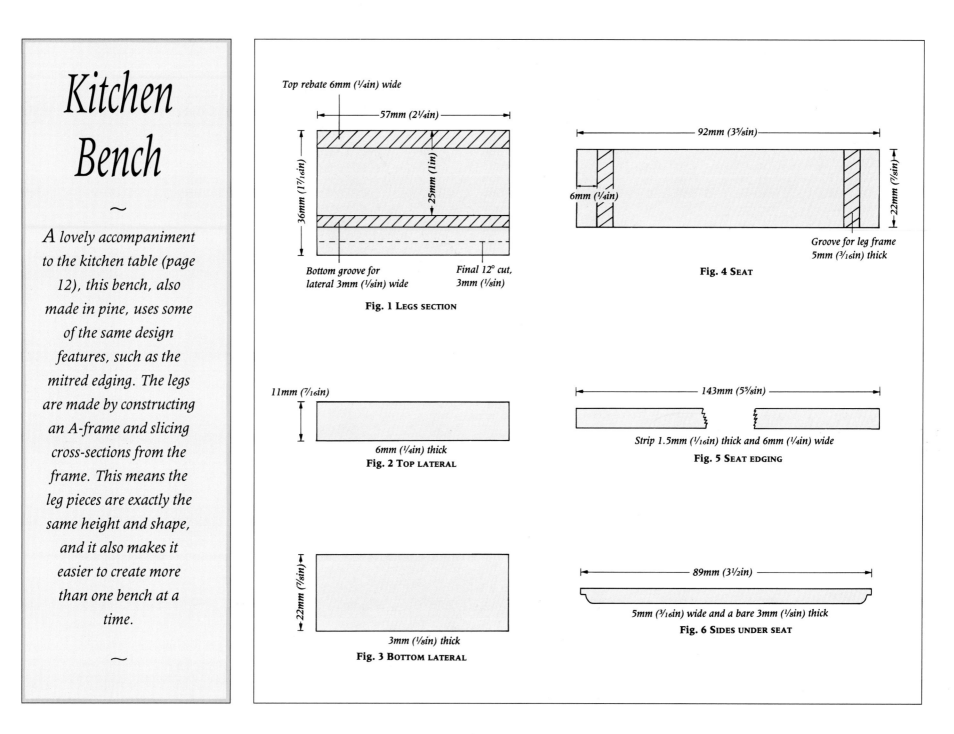

Top rebate 6mm (¼in) wide

57mm (2¼in)

36mm (1⁷⁄₁₆in)

25mm (1in)

Bottom groove for lateral 3mm (⅛in) wide

Final 12° cut, 3mm (⅛in)

Fig. 1 LEGS SECTION

11mm (⁷⁄₁₆in)

6mm (¼in) thick

Fig. 2 TOP LATERAL

22mm (⁷⁄₈in)

3mm (⅛in) thick

Fig. 3 BOTTOM LATERAL

92mm (3⅝in)

6mm (¼in)

22mm (⁷⁄₈in)

Groove for leg frame 5mm (³⁄₁₆in) thick

Fig. 4 SEAT

143mm (5⅝in)

Strip 1.5mm (¹⁄₁₆in) thick and 6mm (¼in) wide

Fig. 5 SEAT EDGING

89mm (3½in)

5mm (³⁄₁₆in) wide and a bare 3mm (⅛in) thick

Fig. 6 SIDES UNDER SEAT

1

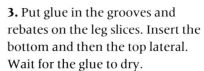

3

1. Cross-cut a section 37 × 25 × 25mm (1⁷⁄₁₆ × 1 × 1in). From this section cut two strips 3mm (⅛in) thick across the grain. Cut a 3mm (⅛in) groove 25mm (1in) from the edge and at a 12° angle. Cut a 6mm (¼in) wide rebate, also at a 12° angle, along the opposite side of the strips. Make the final cut (see Fig. 1) at a 12° angle.

2. Cut the two lateral pieces (see Figs. 2 and 3).

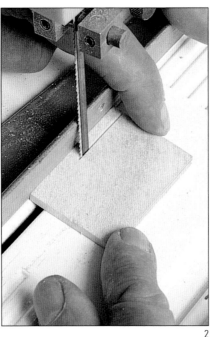

2

4

3. Put glue in the grooves and rebates on the leg slices. Insert the bottom and then the top lateral. Wait for the glue to dry.

4. Slice off the leg frames as cross-sections 5mm (³⁄₁₆in) thick.

5. Cut the bench seat (see Fig. 4). Cut 5mm (³⁄₁₆in) wide grooves in the underside to take the leg frames. Cut two seat edging strips (see Fig. 5). Mitre and glue the edgings to the seat.

6. Glue the leg frames into the grooves in the seat.

7. Cut two strips and mould them to the shape shown in Fig. 6. Glue these strips to the underside of the bench. Sand and wax the top surface and edges of the seat, the leg frame and one side of the bench sides.

5

6

7

Pine Corner Cupboard

~

The clever construction of this cupboard – slicing the shelves from a triangular block – will ensure that all the shelves are exactly the same size, that the back pieces fit properly and that the cupboard will fit into the corner snugly. The moulded pieces at the top and bottom, and the shaped shelf fronts add a decorative touch.

~

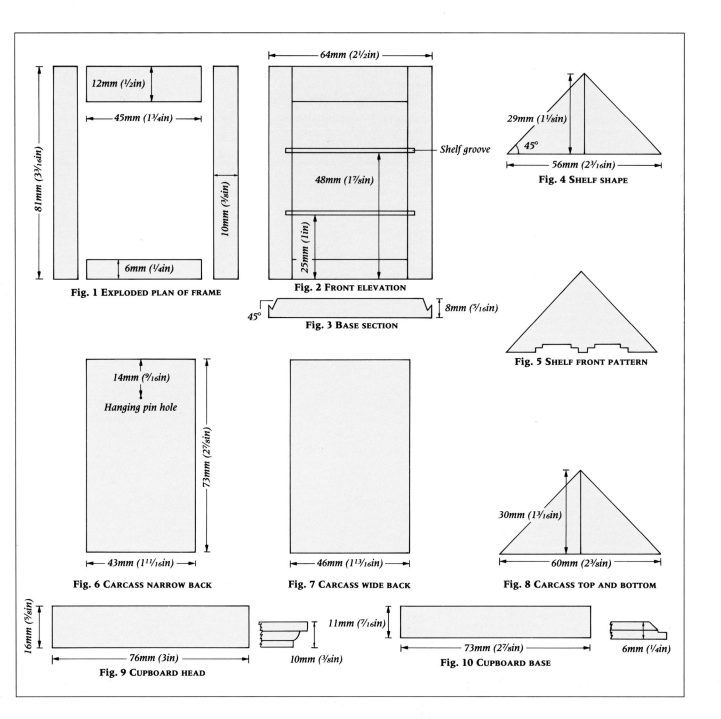

12mm (½in)

45mm (1¾in)

81mm (3³⁄₁₆in)

10mm (⅜in)

6mm (¼in)

Fig. 1 EXPLODED PLAN OF FRAME

64mm (2½in)

Shelf groove

48mm (1⅞in)

25mm (1in)

Fig. 2 FRONT ELEVATION

45°   8mm (⁵⁄₁₆in)

Fig. 3 BASE SECTION

29mm (1⅛in)

45°

56mm (2³⁄₁₆in)

Fig. 4 SHELF SHAPE

Fig. 5 SHELF FRONT PATTERN

14mm (⁹⁄₁₆in)

Hanging pin hole

73mm (2⅞in)

43mm (1¹¹⁄₁₆in)

Fig. 6 CARCASS NARROW BACK

46mm (1¹³⁄₁₆in)

Fig. 7 CARCASS WIDE BACK

30mm (1³⁄₁₆in)

60mm (2⅜in)

Fig. 8 CARCASS TOP AND BOTTOM

16mm (⅝in)

76mm (3in)

Fig. 9 CUPBOARD HEAD

10mm (⅜in)

11mm (⁷⁄₁₆in)

73mm (2⅞in)

6mm (¼in)

Fig. 10 CUPBOARD BASE

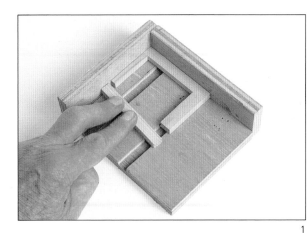

1

1. Cut the components of the basic frame 8mm (5/16in) thick (see Fig. 1). Assemble and glue the frame together.

2

2. Cut the base section, as shown in Fig. 3, to a 45° angle. Cut two 3mm (1/8in) grooves in the frame for the shelves. Sand and wax the front and side edges.

4. Shape the front of the triangular block as shown in Fig. 5.

5. Slice shelves from the block to the width of the shelf grooves already cut. Assemble the shelves in the carcass.

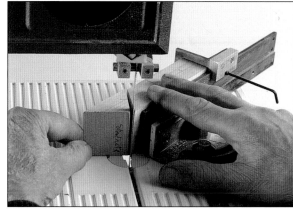

3

3. Cut a section 38 × 18 × 150mm (1½ × ¾ × 6in) along the grain.

Cut a triangular block from this section to make the shelves (see Fig. 4). Keep any remaining pieces to form the top and bottom of the carcass.

4

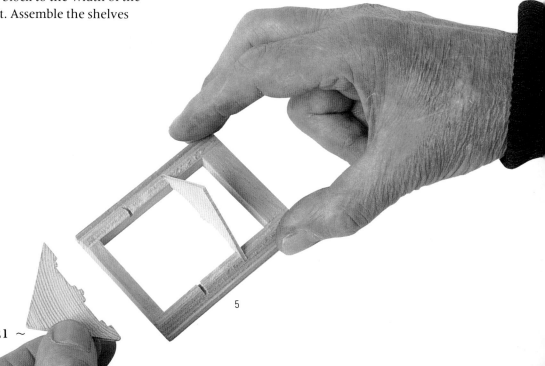

5

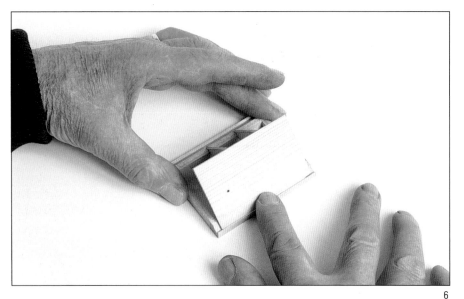

6

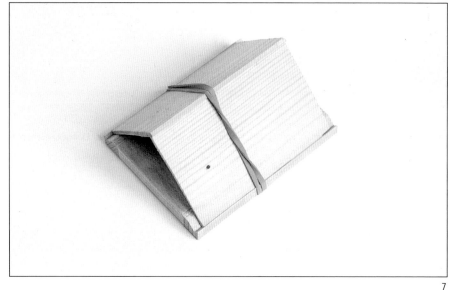

7

6. Cut pieces for the carcass back 1.5mm (¹⁄₁₆in) thick. Drill the hanging holes in the narrower piece. (see Figs. 6 and 7.) Fit the narrow piece first.

7. Use an elastic band to hold the back pieces in place.

8

8. Cut the top and bottom pieces (Fig. 8) from the block made in step 3. Fit and glue the base and top in position.

9

9. Cut blanks for the cupboard head and base. Mould the fronts and ends. (see Figs. 9 and 10.)

10. Make a 45° cut to the corners of the base and head pieces. This cut will be 5mm (³⁄₁₆in) from the front edge of these pieces. Sand and wax the base and heads.

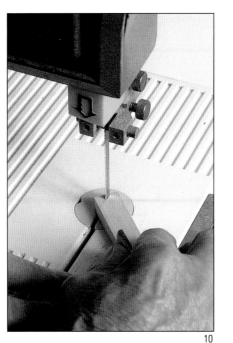

10

11. Glue the base and head in place. Cut a pad 12mm (½in) square and 6mm (¼in) deep and glue it to the underside of the carcass.

11

Note
~

Each time you make this cupboard, it will have slightly different measurements. The measurements in Fig. 2 form the basis for all subsequent measurements; all pieces made after the basic frame should be measured against the frame and cut to fit; the measurements given are approximate.

Pine Hanging Shelves

~

A decorative but useful piece for any kitchen, these shelves work best in pine since the light colour and simple designs complement the bright colours used in many kitchens. The small drawers beneath the bottom shelf are constructed in exactly the same way as the drawers in the other projects.

~

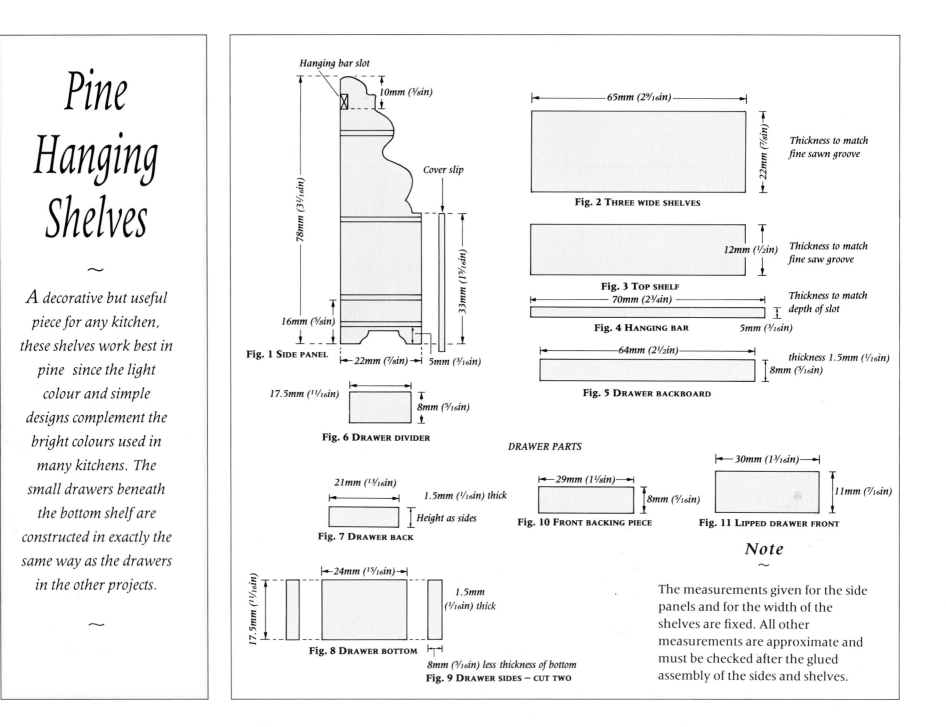

Hanging bar slot

10mm (³⁄₈in)

Cover slip

78mm (3¹⁄₁₆in)

33mm (1⁵⁄₁₆in)

16mm (⁵⁄₈in)

Fig. 1 SIDE PANEL

22mm (⁷⁄₈in)   5mm (³⁄₁₆in)

65mm (2⁹⁄₁₆in)

22mm (⁷⁄₈in)

Thickness to match fine sawn groove

Fig. 2 THREE WIDE SHELVES

12mm (¹⁄₂in)   Thickness to match fine saw groove

Fig. 3 TOP SHELF

70mm (2³⁄₄in)   Thickness to match depth of slot

Fig. 4 HANGING BAR   5mm (³⁄₁₆in)

64mm (2¹⁄₂in)   thickness 1.5mm (¹⁄₁₆in)

8mm (⁵⁄₁₆in)

Fig. 5 DRAWER BACKBOARD

17.5mm (¹¹⁄₁₆in)   8mm (⁵⁄₁₆in)

Fig. 6 DRAWER DIVIDER

DRAWER PARTS

21mm (¹³⁄₁₆in)   1.5mm (¹⁄₁₆in) thick

Height as sides

Fig. 7 DRAWER BACK

29mm (1¹⁄₈in)   8mm (⁵⁄₁₆in)

Fig. 10 FRONT BACKING PIECE

30mm (1³⁄₁₆in)   11mm (⁷⁄₁₆in)

Fig. 11 LIPPED DRAWER FRONT

24mm (¹⁵⁄₁₆in)   1.5mm (¹⁄₁₆in) thick

17.5mm (¹¹⁄₁₆in)

Fig. 8 DRAWER BOTTOM

8mm (⁵⁄₁₆in) less thickness of bottom

Fig. 9 DRAWER SIDES – CUT TWO

Note

~

The measurements given for the side panels and for the width of the shelves are fixed. All other measurements are approximate and must be checked after the glued assembly of the sides and shelves.

1

1. You will need a section 22mm (⁷/₈in) wide and 81mm (3³/₁₆in) long and sufficiently deep to provide slices for the sides, the shelves and the cover slips. Cut generous 78 × 22 × 1.5mm (3¹/₁₆ × ⁷/₈ × ¹/₁₆in) slices for the side pieces. Run grooves to the measurements shown in Fig. 1.

2. Draw the pattern onto the sides. If you are cutting more than one set of sides, you can pin several slices together and cut all the sides in one go (see *pinning blanks*). Cut the hanging bar slot in the sides.

2

3

3. Make the moulded cuts for the feet.

4

4. Cut out the pattern.

5. Slice two cover slips from the blank already made and cut them to 33mm (1⁵⁄₁₆in) long. Glue the cover strips to the sides. They should be flush with the top edge of the front and protrude by 3mm (¹⁄₈in) at the bottom, where they are trimmed off with a craft knife.

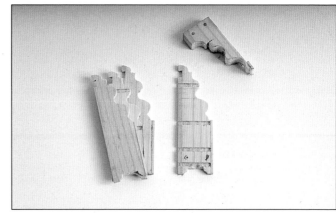

5

6

6. The unpinned block, showing the sides with pattern and grooves cut.

7. Cut four slices from the section made in step 1 for the shelves. Reduce the width of one slice to match the depth of the top shelf groove. Cut all the shelves to a finished length of 65mm (2⁹⁄₁₆in) (see Figs. 2 and 3). Sand and wax the visible surfaces. Glue the shelves to the side panels on the jig.

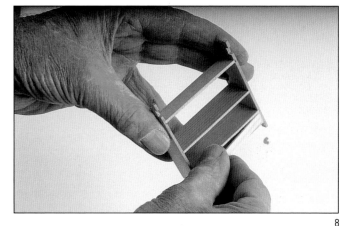

7

8

8. Cut the drawer backboard (see Fig. 5) and test for fit against the carcass. Sand and wax.

9. Cut the drawer divider (see Fig. 6) and test for fit. Sand and wax.

10. Cut the hanging bar (see Fig. 4) and make the holes marked, test for fit and then sand and wax it. Make sure the ends of the hanging bar are flush with the sides.

9

10

11

11. Cut, sand and wax the drawer components (see Figs. 7–11). Apply glue to the front edge of the bottom piece and glue to the front piece. Apply glue to the front and bottom of the right side. Leave glue to set and then assemble left side in the same way. Test for fit against the assembled carcass. The lipped drawer front should overlap the top, bottom and sides by about 1.5mm (¹⁄₁₆in).

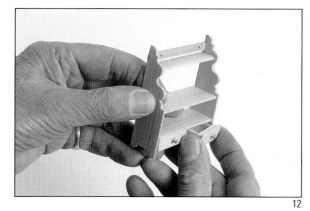

12

12. Make small holes in the drawer fronts for the knobs, apply glue and insert. Place the carcass on its back and leave to dry overnight.

Mantel Clock

~

This is a replica of a German doll's house clock dating from the 1840s.

You Will Need

~

- Hard wood for clock body 25 × 16 × 16mm (1 × ⅝ × ⅝in); for base 25 × 16 × 3mm (1 × ⅝ × ⅛in); for pediment 12 × 16 × 10mm (1 × ⅝ × ⅜in); for feet, 4 pieces, each 6 × 6 × 3mm (¼ × ¼ × ⅛in)
- Fine sandpaper
- Matt enamel paint (black) or mahogany wood stain and French polish
- Thin bone knitting needle or ivory-painted cocktail stick, cut into 4 pieces, each 16mm (⅝in)
- Large, flat-headed drawing pin
- Small paper printed clock face (draw or photocopy the example shown here)
- Clear varnish
- Wood glue
- Superglue gel
- Gloss enamel paint (ivory), if needed for pillars

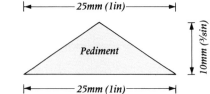

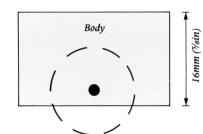

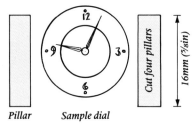

Pillar   Sample dial

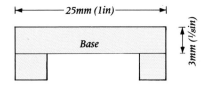

All pieces 12mm (½in) deep

1. Cut out the pieces of wood. Smooth all surfaces with fine sandpaper and finish all visible surfaces with either mahogany wood stain and French polish to imitate the rosewood antique version or with matt black enamel paint.

2. Glue the pediment to the clock body. Back the clock face with card and glue it to the head of the drawing pin. Varnish it. Drill a hole in the clock body with a fine spiral drill. Put some glue on the shank of the pin and push it firmly into the hole. Using a drill will prevent the wood from splitting.

3. Glue the feet to the clock base. Set the pillars at each corner of the base, press each one firmly in a dab of glue onto the base and allow to set. Apply a spot of glue to the tops of the pillar and stand the clock body in place on the pillars, making sure that the body and base are aligned. Press firmly in place and leave to dry.

The Bedroom

~

Bed

~

This design is one of the simplest in terms of the number of components. However, you will still need to work as carefully and accurately as possible. As with any piece with separate legs, you will have to be especially careful to ensure all the legs are level. You could shape the bed head to any design you wish – perhaps a simple rounded shape.

~

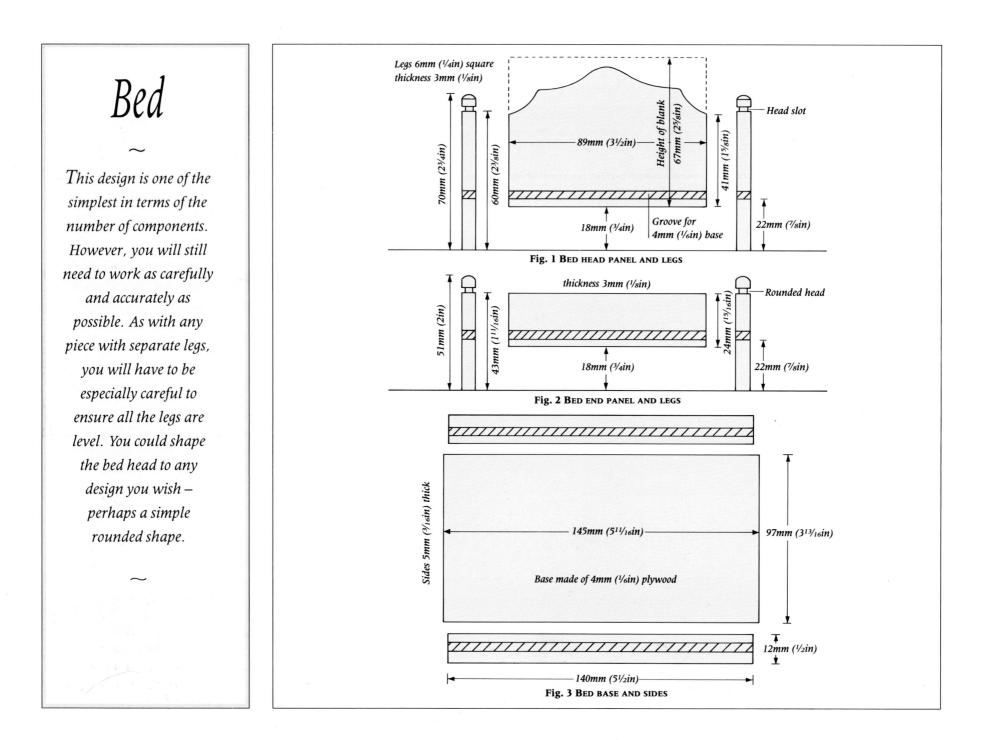

Fig. 1 BED HEAD PANEL AND LEGS

Fig. 2 BED END PANEL AND LEGS

Fig. 3 BED BASE AND SIDES

1. Cut out four pine legs. Make slots in the heads and round the tops (see Fig. 1).

2. Take a piece of pine to the dimensions shown in Fig. 1 for the headboard. Make a line down the middle and draw in the headboard shape, making sure the pattern is exactly symmetrical about the centre line. Cut the headboard out.

3. Cut the end panel out (see Fig. 2). Sand, seal and wax both panels.

4. Assemble the legs and the headboard by butting them together and fixing with glue. The top edge of each panel should be slightly below the bottom edge of the leg head slots. Allow the glue to set. Repeat for the legs and the end panel.

5. Cut 4mm (⅙in) base grooves in both the assembled panels.

5

7

6. Make some "stops" to fill the grooves and stop the base board moving. They need to be the depth of the groove and a bare 5mm (³⁄₁₆in) long. Glue the stops no more than 3mm (⅛in) into the groove and running with the grain. Test the distance between the stops with a ruler – they must be at least 97mm (3¹³⁄₁₆in) apart for the base to fit easily. Sand down the stops so they are flush with the leg surface. Sand, seal and wax the legs.

6

7. Dry-assemble the base to the head and end panels. Measure the distance between the head legs and end legs. Cut the base side pieces (see Fig. 3) so that they are very slightly longer than this measurement. Cut a 4mm (⅙in) groove in each side.

8. Sand, seal and wax the sides. Use a cocktail stick to put glue in the side grooves and offer the sides to the base so that the base protrudes equally at both sides.

8

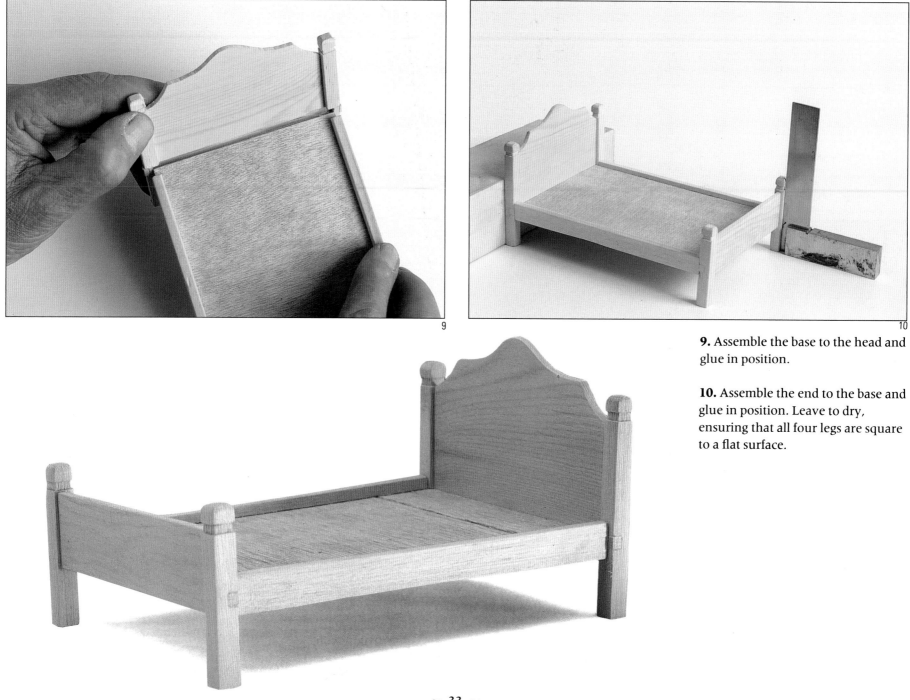

9. Assemble the base to the head and glue in position.

10. Assemble the end to the base and glue in position. Leave to dry, ensuring that all four legs are square to a flat surface.

Bedside Table

~

This simple but charming design is an essential piece in any bedroom, and it complements the pine bed (see page 30) perfectly. The feet are shaped by cutting out semi- and quarter circles, as are the lateral pieces beneath the table top. The legs are made of lengths of dowel.

~

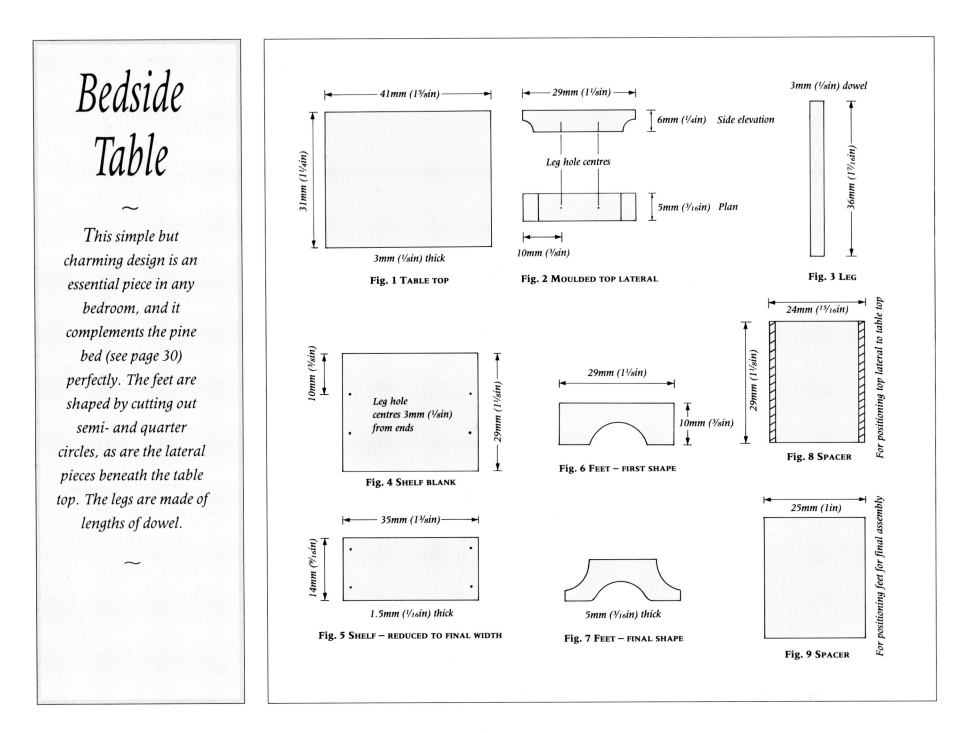

41mm (1⅝in)

31mm (1¼in)

3mm (⅛in) thick

Fig. 1 TABLE TOP

29mm (1⅛in)

6mm (¼in) Side elevation

Leg hole centres

5mm (³⁄₁₆in) Plan

10mm (⅜in)

Fig. 2 MOULDED TOP LATERAL

3mm (⅛in) dowel

36mm (1⁷⁄₁₆in)

Fig. 3 LEG

10mm (⅜in)

Leg hole centres 3mm (⅛in) from ends

29mm (1⅛in)

Fig. 4 SHELF BLANK

35mm (1⅜in)

14mm (⁹⁄₁₆in)

1.5mm (¹⁄₁₆in) thick

Fig. 5 SHELF – REDUCED TO FINAL WIDTH

29mm (1⅛in)

10mm (⅜in)

Fig. 6 FEET – FIRST SHAPE

5mm (³⁄₁₆in) thick

Fig. 7 FEET – FINAL SHAPE

24mm (1⁵⁄₁₆in)

29mm (1⅛in)

Fig. 8 SPACER

For positioning top lateral to table top

25mm (1in)

Fig. 9 SPACER

For positioning feet for final assembly

1. All the pieces shown are cut from pine except the two spacers (Figs. 8 and 9), which are cut from scrap wood. For the feet, cut two blanks 29 × 10 × 5mm (1⅛ × ⅜ × ³⁄₁₆in). To shape the feet, first hollow out the centre semi-circle.

2. Hollow out two quarter-circles from either side to form the final shape of the feet.

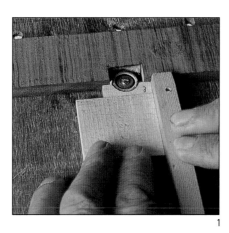

1

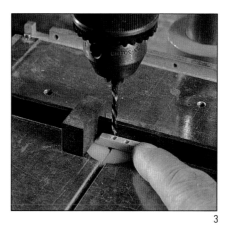

3

3. Cut two top lateral pieces 29 × 6mm (1⅛ × ¼in) and 5mm (³⁄₁₆in) wide, and mould to the shape shown (see Fig. 2). These pieces sit underneath the table top at the top of the legs. Drill two holes for the legs, each 10mm (⅜in) from the end of the lateral.

4. To make the shelf, cut a section 29mm (1⅛in) wide and at least 51mm (2in) long. Cut along the grain so that it is barely 3mm (⅛in) thick. Trim the section down so that it is 35mm (1⅜in) long. Make four leg holes 10mm (⅜in) from the edge as shown in Fig. 4.

4

2

5

5. Reduce the width of the shelf to 14mm (⁹⁄₁₆in), which is the length of the flat surface of the feet pieces minus 1.5mm (¹⁄₁₆in). You may have to do this by a process of trial and error. The holes in the shelf must be equidistant from both sides.

8. Put some glue on the underside of the table top and attach it, using the spacer to ensure accuracy. Put some glue on the top, flat surface of the feet and glue them to the shelf so that the feet pieces are in line with the shelf ends and the shelf is centred over the feet pieces. Use the 25mm (1in) wide spacer to position the feet in the final assembly.

6. Cut the top piece (Fig. 1). Hand sand and wax the top surfaces and edges of the table top and shelf, the legs, the outside surface and moulding of the top lateral and the side surfaces and shaping of the feet

pieces. Take four pieces of 3mm (⅛in) dowel (Fig. 3), insert some glue into the holes in the shelf and push in the legs. Check that the ends are flush with the underside of the shelf.

7. Cut the wide spacer and run "anti-glue" rebates down either side, as shown in Fig. 8. Place the table top upside-down on an assembly jig. Place the spacer on top. Put glue in the holes in the laterals and insert the legs. Check that the shelf is in line with the table top edge. Remove the table top. Check the shelf is parallel to the jig floor; check the legs are vertical from the end and the front. Allow the glued legs to dry.

Chest of Drawers

~

This piece is made of mahogany-style wood, but could just as easily be made from pine, depending on your decoration scheme. The feet are not separate components, but are simply formed by shaping the bottom edge of the sides and the front apron. All the visible surfaces – the back is made of plywood – will need to be finished thoroughly, using several coats of polish.

~

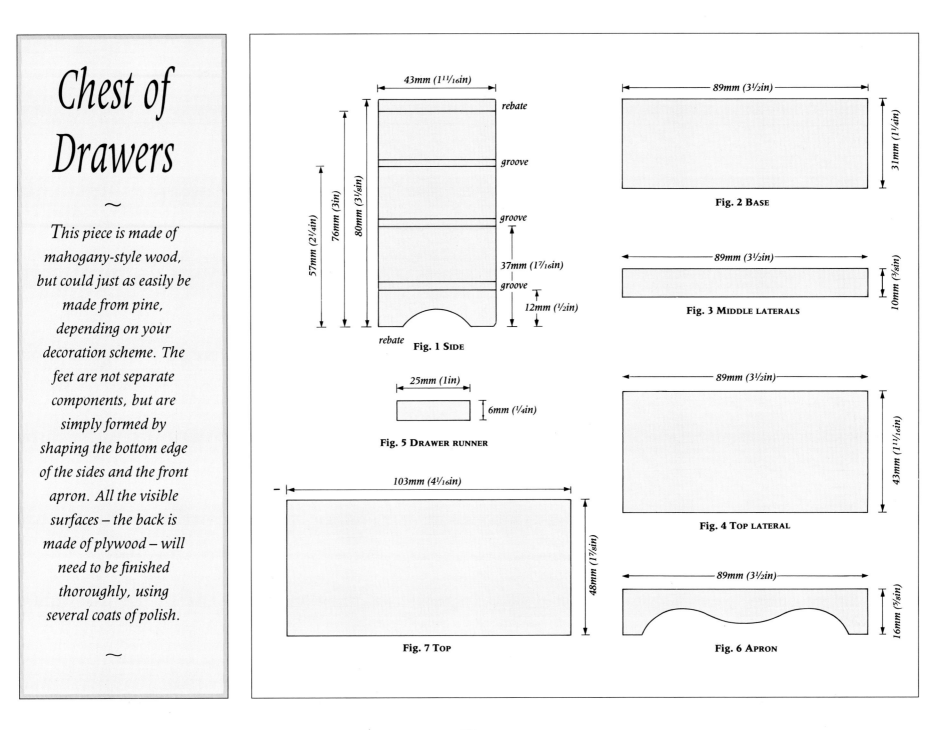

43mm (1¹¹/₁₆in)

rebate

groove

groove

groove

57mm (2¹/₄in)

76mm (3in)

80mm (3¹/₈in)

37mm (1⁷/₁₆in)

12mm (¹/₂in)

rebate

Fig. 1 SIDE

25mm (1in)

6mm (¹/₄in)

Fig. 5 DRAWER RUNNER

103mm (4¹/₁₆in)

48mm (1⁷/₈in)

Fig. 7 TOP

89mm (3¹/₂in)

31mm (1¹/₄in)

Fig. 2 BASE

89mm (3¹/₂in)

10mm (³/₈in)

Fig. 3 MIDDLE LATERALS

89mm (3¹/₂in)

43mm (1¹¹/₁₆in)

Fig. 4 TOP LATERAL

89mm (3¹/₂in)

16mm (⁵/₈in)

Fig. 6 APRON

1. You will need a section of wood 51 × 95 × 45mm (2 × 3¾ × 1¾in). From this you can cut two sides, one top lateral, two middle laterals, one base and four drawer runners. For the sides, cut off two slices to the dimensions shown in Fig. 1. Cut three grooves about 3mm (⅛in) wide for the middle laterals and one rebate 3mm (⅛in) wide for the top lateral. Cut a rebate down each side to hold the back.

2. To form the feet, cut out a semi-circle as shown in Fig. 1. Measure the depth of the grooves and rebate. Cut out the base, one top lateral, two middle laterals and four drawer runners (Figs. 2–5), making the width match the depth of the grooves and rebate. Cut the back (Fig. 8) from 4mm (⅙in) plywood and test for fit against the side rebate.

3. Make plugs for the front ends of the grooves cut for the base. Cut pieces to the depth of the groove and about 5mm (³⁄₁₆in) long. Glue the stops to the grooves so that they protrude slightly at the front. Hand sand the inner and front sides so that the plugs are flush. Sand, stain and polish the front edges and sides, and the middle and top laterals.

1

2

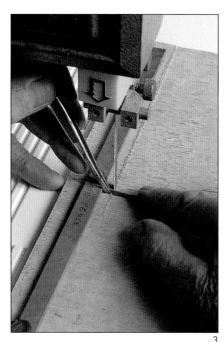

3

4. Assemble the drawer runners. Position the back end of the runners flush with the rebate for the back. Put glue in the grooves and insert the runners, using a small piece of wood to check that they are vertical.

4

5

6

5. Assemble the carcass. Put glue in the grooves and rebates on the sides. Place the left side on an assembly jig with the feet pressed against the jig wall. Assemble the back so that its top matches the top of the side.

6. Assemble the base flush to the rebate wall. Assemble the right side and the top lateral.

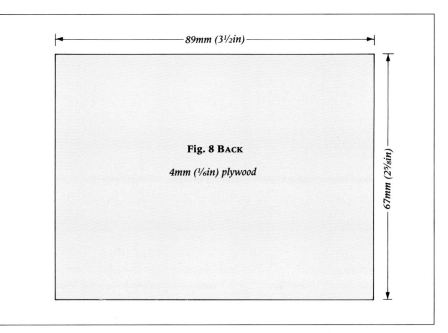

|←————— 89mm (3½in) —————→|

Fig. 8 BACK

4mm (⅛in) plywood

↕ 67mm (2⅝in)

7

7. Assemble the middle laterals and the ends, which should be flush with the front edges of the sides.

8. Cut a section 16mm (⅝in) wide along the grain and 12 × 92mm (½ × 3⅝in). Measure the distance between the sides of the assembled carcass to determine the width of the apron. Cut out the apron to the shape shown in Fig. 6. If you want to ensure a really snug fit, first cut out the apron in 4mm (⅙in) plywood and test it for fit.

9. Sand, stain and polish the front of the apron. Slice the section so that it is slightly less thick than the distance between the front edges of the sides and base. Fit the apron.

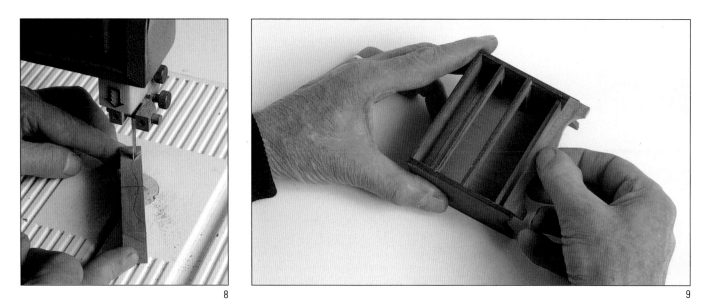

8

9

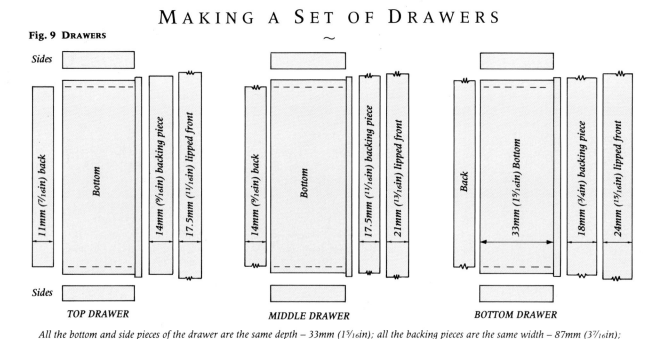

MAKING A SET OF DRAWERS

~

Fig. 9 DRAWERS

Sides

11mm (⁷⁄₁₆in) back
Bottom
14mm (⁹⁄₁₆in) backing piece
17.5mm (¹¹⁄₁₆in) lipped front

Sides

TOP DRAWER

14mm (⁹⁄₁₆in) back
Bottom
17.5mm (¹¹⁄₁₆in) backing piece
21mm (¹³⁄₁₆in) lipped front

MIDDLE DRAWER

Back
33mm (1⁵⁄₁₆in) Bottom
18mm (¾in) backing piece
24mm (1⁵⁄₁₆in) lipped front

BOTTOM DRAWER

All the bottom and side pieces of the drawer are the same depth – 33mm (1⁵⁄₁₆in); all the backing pieces are the same width – 87mm (3⁷⁄₁₆in); and all the lipped fronts are the same width – 90mm (3⁹⁄₁₆in).

Assemble the drawers by placing the drawer front backing piece against the vertical back of a basic assembly jig. Apply glue to the front of the drawer bottom and to the backing piece. Apply glue to the front and the bottom of the right-hand side as you look at it. Holding a small square of wood in your right hand, press it against the edge of the drawer bottom and side so that they line up exactly. Push the side against the backing piece. Allow the glue to set. Assemble the left-hand side. Fit the back. Fit the lipped drawer front, which should overlap the drawer opening top, bottom and sides by about 1.5mm (¹⁄₁₆in). Sand, stain and polish the drawer fronts and leave to dry overnight.

10

10. Mark out where the knobs will go – about 18mm (¾in) from the edge. Make the holes, apply some glue to the knobs and insert. Remove the drawers. Sand, stain and polish the carcass sides. Cut the top (Fig. 4) and glue it to the carcass. Sand, stain and polish the top. Leave to dry overnight.

Dressing Table

~

This is one of three carcasses similar in their basic structure; the others are the desk and the sideboard. The structure of the drawers, and of course the number of grooves and rebates required to hold the drawers, differ but once you have mastered one design, you will be able to complete the other two without difficulty.

~

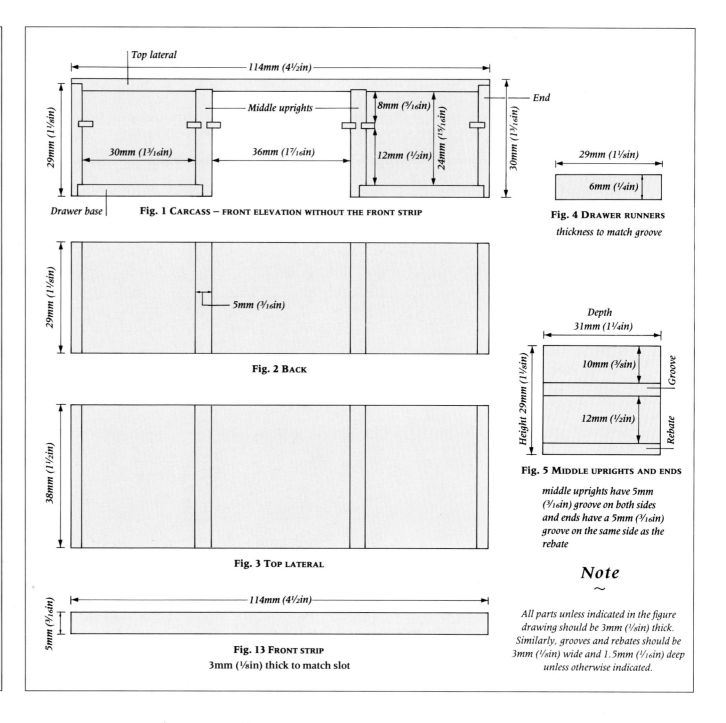

Top lateral

114mm (4½in)

Middle uprights

8mm (³/₁₆in)

End

29mm (1⅛in)

30mm (1³/₁₆in)   36mm (1⁷/₁₆in)   12mm (½in)   24mm (1⁵/₁₆in)   30mm (1³/₁₆in)

Drawer base

Fig. 1 CARCASS – FRONT ELEVATION WITHOUT THE FRONT STRIP

29mm (1⅛in)

6mm (¼in)

Fig. 4 DRAWER RUNNERS
thickness to match groove

29mm (1⅛in)

5mm (³/₁₆in)

Fig. 2 BACK

Depth
31mm (1¼in)

10mm (³/₈in)   Groove

Height 29mm (1⅛in)

12mm (½in)   Rebate

Fig. 5 MIDDLE UPRIGHTS AND ENDS

middle uprights have 5mm (³/₁₆in) groove on both sides and ends have a 5mm (³/₁₆in) groove on the same side as the rebate

38mm (1½in)

Fig. 3 TOP LATERAL

Note

~

All parts unless indicated in the figure drawing should be 3mm (⅛in) thick. Similarly, grooves and rebates should be 3mm (⅛in) wide and 1.5mm (¹/₁₆in) deep unless otherwise indicated.

5mm (³/₁₆in)

114mm (4½in)

Fig. 13 FRONT STRIP
3mm (⅛in) thick to match slot

1

1. Cut out the back from 4mm (⅛in) plywood. Cut out the top lateral, two middle uprights and two ends from your chosen wood. Cut the grooves and rebates in the back and top lateral as indicated on Figs. 2 and 3.

2. Cut rebates and grooves in the middle uprights and ends (see Fig. 5). Middle upright grooves should be 5mm (³⁄₁₆in) wide. Cut six drawer runners of a thickness to match the grooves (Fig. 4).

2

3

3. Holding the top lateral and back together, insert the middle uprights into the grooves and glue in place. Use a cocktail stick to put glue in the drawer runner grooves on the middle uprights and insert four drawer runners. Make sure the ends of the drawer runners butt against the back and leave a gap of 5mm (³⁄₁₆in) at the front for the front strip.

4. Insert the ends into the grooves and glue in place. Glue the two remaining drawer runners into the ends, again making sure the runners butt against the back and that there is a 5mm (³⁄₁₆in) gap at the front.

4

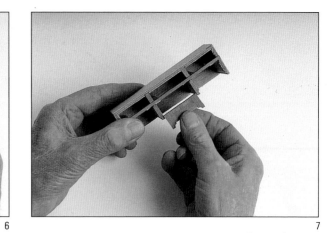

5. Cut a groove 5mm (³/₁₆in) deep and 3mm (⅛in) wide right the way across the front of the carcass; this must exactly match the position of the grooves for the drawer runners.

6. Cut the front strip (Fig. 13) and glue it into the groove in the front of the carcass. Belt or hand sand the ends and bottom of the carcass with medium sandpaper on a flat surface. The ends must be flush for gluing to the end panels and protrusions at the bottom will look untidy.

7. Make the apron from three pieces of wood as illustrated in Fig. 6, taking careful note of the direction of the grain on each piece. The final thickness of the apron needs to be 3mm (⅛in). Fit and glue the apron to the carcass.

8. Cut two side drawer bases (Fig. 7) and glue them in place in the carcass. Sand, stain and French polish the front of the carcass (see page 9).

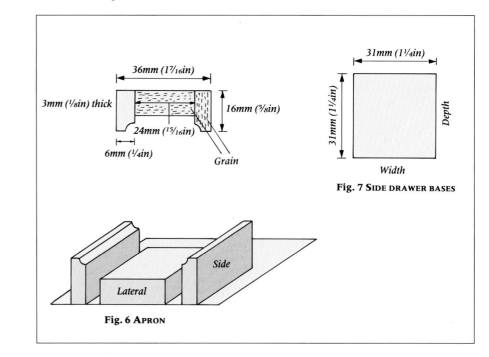

36mm (1⁷/₁₆in)

3mm (⅛in) thick

16mm (⅝in)

24mm (¹⁵/₁₆in)

6mm (¼in)

Grain

31mm (1¼in)

31mm (1¼in)

Depth

Width

Fig. 7 SIDE DRAWER BASES

Side

Lateral

Fig. 6 APRON

MAKING THE LEGS
~

9. The completed carcass.

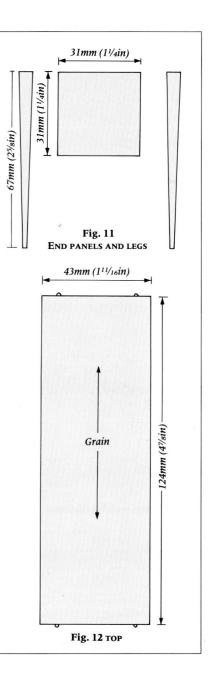

Fig. 11
END PANELS AND LEGS

31mm (1¼in)
31mm (1¼in)
67mm (2⅝in)

43mm (1¹¹⁄₁₆in)
124mm (4⅞in)
Grain

Fig. 12 TOP

10. Cut four legs and taper them to the measurements shown in Fig. 11 using medium sandpaper. Fine sand, stain and polish the legs. Cut two end panels to a bare 3mm (⅛in) thick (Fig. 11). Sand, stain and polish one side. Fit the legs to the panels and assemble on a jig. The polish should be scraped off the areas to be glued. Make sure the leg tops and the top edge of the panel are exactly aligned.

11. Cut the carcass top (Fig. 12) and glue it to the carcass. Position, but do not glue, the assembled end panels and check that the overhang of the top is equal. Check that the back of the table top aligns with the back of the carcass. Remove the end panels. Sand, stain and polish the top. Glue the end panels in position. The back legs should be in line with the back and the front legs should protrude slightly.

MAKING A SET OF DRAWERS

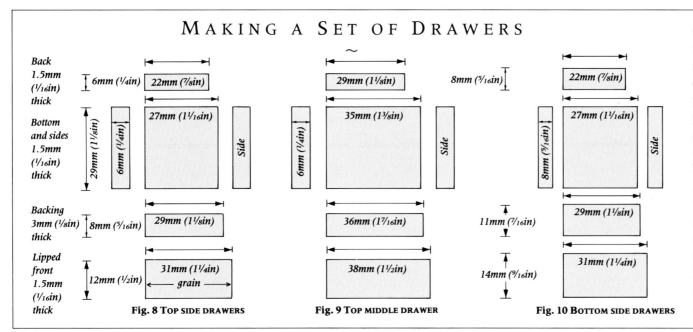

Back
1.5mm
(1/16in)
thick

6mm (1/4in) | 22mm (7/8in)

29mm (1 1/8in)

**Bottom
and sides**
1.5mm
(1/16in)
thick

6mm (1/4in) | 27mm (1 1/16in) | Side

Backing
3mm (1/8in)
thick

8mm (5/16in) | 29mm (1 1/8in)

**Lipped
front**
1.5mm
(1/16in)
thick

12mm (1/2in) | 31mm (1 1/4in)
grain

Fig. 8 TOP SIDE DRAWERS

~

29mm (1 1/8in)

8mm (5/16in)

35mm (1 3/8in)

6mm (1/4in) | | Side

36mm (1 7/16in)

38mm (1 1/2in)

Fig. 9 TOP MIDDLE DRAWER

22mm (7/8in)

27mm (1 1/16in) | Side

8mm (5/16in)

11mm (7/16in)

14mm (9/16in)

29mm (1 1/8in)

31mm (1 1/4in)

Fig. 10 BOTTOM SIDE DRAWERS

Cut out the drawer components – two top side drawers, two bottom side drawers and one top middle drawer. Assemble the drawers by placing the drawer front backing piece against the back of an assembly jig. Apply glue to the front of the drawer bottom and to the backing piece. Allow the glue to set. Assemble the left side in the same way. Fit the drawers to the carcass. Attach the lipped front. Sand the drawer fronts with medium and fine sandpaper, dust, stain and polish. Drill holes for the knobs, insert some glue and insert the knobs. Leave to dry overnight on its back.

Shell Mirror

This mirror is a replica of a Victorian novelty.

You Will Need
~

- ☛ Card or thin wood (aero-ply), 57 × 29mm (2½ × 1⅛in)
- ☛ Marbled paper to cover
- ☛ White glue
- ☛ Thin mirror or foil, 25 × 25mm (1 × 1in)
- ☛ 16 mouse-ear shells
- ☛ 9–10 assorted tiny, pretty shells of various shapes
- ☛ Gold felt-tipped pen for outlining handle (optional)
- ☛ 38mm (1½in) narrow ribbon, 3mm (⅛in) wide for hanging loop

1. Cut out the shape in wood or strong card. Pierce a hole in the handle.

2. Place the shape on marbled paper. Draw around it, leaving a margin all round of about 3mm (⅛in) for the backing. Draw a second pattern but to the exact shape for the front cover.

3. Glue the card or wood shape firmly to the backing paper. Smooth it with a dry, clean cloth and glue the overlap allowance down firmly on the front surface,

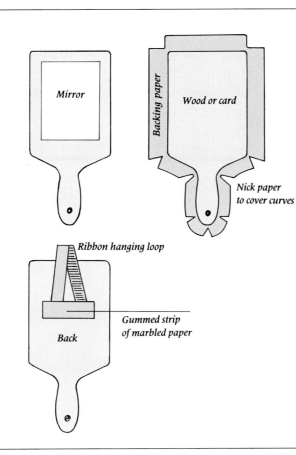

Mirror

Backing paper

Wood or card

Nick paper to cover curves

Ribbon hanging loop

Gummed strip of marbled paper

Back

nicking it with scissors on the curves.

4. Glue the front paper piece firmly in position, smoothing it with a clean, dry cloth. Glue the mirror in position on the front.

5. Make a rough pattern of the template in plain paper and arrange the shells on it until you are happy with the design, then transfer the shells one by one to the actual mirror rim.

6. Run glue along the top edge of the mirror backing and, starting at the centre, press the shells into position. Continue down the sides and along the bottom edge.

7. Outline the handle in gold.

8. Pierce through the hole in the handle. Fix a small hanging loop of ribbon on the back with a piece of marbled paper if you want to hang it up.

Doll's House

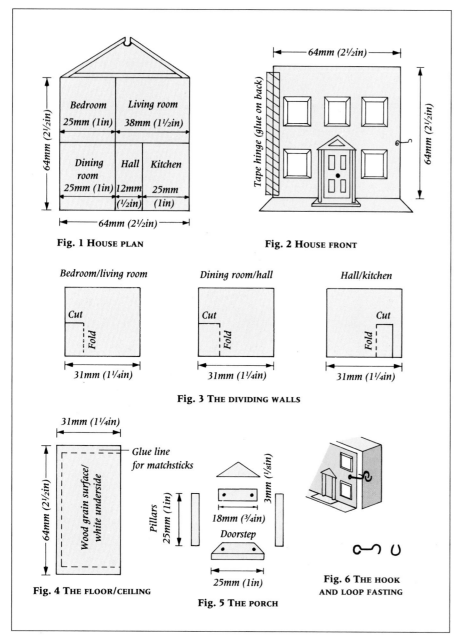

Fig. 1 HOUSE PLAN

Bedroom 25mm (1in)
Living room 38mm (1½in)
Dining room 25mm (1in)
Hall 12mm (½in)
Kitchen 25mm (1in)
64mm (2½in)
64mm (2½in)

Tape hinge (glue on back)
64mm (2½in)
64mm (2½in)

Fig. 2 HOUSE FRONT

Bedroom/living room
Dining room/hall
Hall/kitchen

Cut — Fold
31mm (1¼in)

Cut — Fold
31mm (1¼in)

Cut — Fold
31mm (1¼in)

Fig. 3 THE DIVIDING WALLS

31mm (1¼in)
Glue line for matchsticks
64mm (2½in)
Wood grain surface/white underside

Fig. 4 THE FLOOR/CEILING

Pillars 25mm (1in)
3mm (⅛in)
18mm (¾in)
Doorstep
25mm (1in)

Fig. 5 THE PORCH

Fig. 6 THE HOOK AND LOOP FASTING

You Will Need
~

- Box 64 × 64 × 31mm (2½ × 2½ × 1¼in)
- Card for base 64 × 45mm (2½ × 1¾in)
- Card for pediment and porch roof, 64 × 18mm (2½ × ¾in)
- Poster paint (ochre or grey) for pediment and body of house
- Matchsticks for pediment moulding and windows
- Wood glue
- Card for front, 64 × 64mm (2½ × 2½in)
- Craft knife or scalpel
- Transparent plastic for windows
- Cocktail sticks for pillars
- 6mm (¼in) tape for hinges
- 1 brass bead for door knob
- Wood 38 × 6mm (1½ × ¼in) for step
- Poster paint (black) for base and apron
- Paint (white) for door, mouldings and pillars
- 3 vertical wall dividers 31 × 31mm (1¼ × 1¼in)
- 1 horizontal floor divider 64 × 31mm (2½ × 1¼in)
- Felt-tipped pens for decoration and detail
- Tiny scraps of wallpaper for walls and floor
- Narrow lace for curtains
- Sequins for ceiling roses (optional)
- Paper glue
- Tweezers
- Wire to make door hook
- Pliers or wire cutters

1. Find or make a suitably sized box. Cut a piece of stiff card 57 × 45mm (2¼ × 1¾in) for the base; this is slightly larger than the house itself to form an apron at the front.

2. Trace the pediment from Fig. 1 and paint it ochre or grey. Punch out a circle from the apex and glue white-painted matchsticks in place. Glue the pediment to the top of the box.

3. Trace the front (see Fig. 2), marking the apertures for the door and windows – ignore the pediment, steps, porch and pillars for the time being – and transfer these to the card front. Use a sharp scalpel or craft knife to cut out the windows and the door, retaining the door piece to re-attach with tape. Paint the front ochre or grey. On the other side, glue the transparent plastic over the windows and glue strips of lace down the sides of the windows to represent curtains. Draw on a dado, skirting line and cornice moulding with felt-tipped pen and add an architrave and, if you wish, a crest over the door.

4. With the piece cut out of the door aperture, glue small pieces of card to represent door panels on the front and attach the brass bead as the door knob. Turn over the door and glue tape along the hinge side, leaving half the width of the tape free to glue to the inside surface of the house front. Paint the back of the door any colour you wish and draw on internal panels. Glue the door hinge in place. On the front draw sash glazing bars across the windows with felt-tipped pen and outline the windows. Cut matchstick mouldings for the top of each window and glue in place.

5. Cut and glue the doorstep, the porch roof, the pillars and the pediment. Use felt-tipped pen to add details to these. The house illustrated has white and gold detailing, but you may prefer to use brown or black.

6. Cut the room and floor dividers as in Figs. 3 and 4. Cut away the door edges and fold them back, so that the folds form hinges. Paper and decorate the surfaces as you wish, then glue them in place in the house. You will probably need tweezers to hold the card in place. If you glue matches close to the edges on the underside of the floor/ceiling piece, it will adhere better to the walls. When the interior is finished, glue the front to the box by means of a tape hinge. Disguise the hinge by gluing a paper cover over the box before painting the outside. Varnish the exterior of the house, adding a drop of wood stain to the varnish to give it an "antique" look.

7. Make a tiny wire hook and loop with fine gauge wire and tweezers. Pin the hook into the house front with a short dress-making pin, snipping off the excess shank on the inside with pliers or wire cutters. Make two small holes on the side of the house to accommodate the loop and glue the wire loop in the holes. You will have to bend the hook slightly so that it curves around the corner.

Cradle

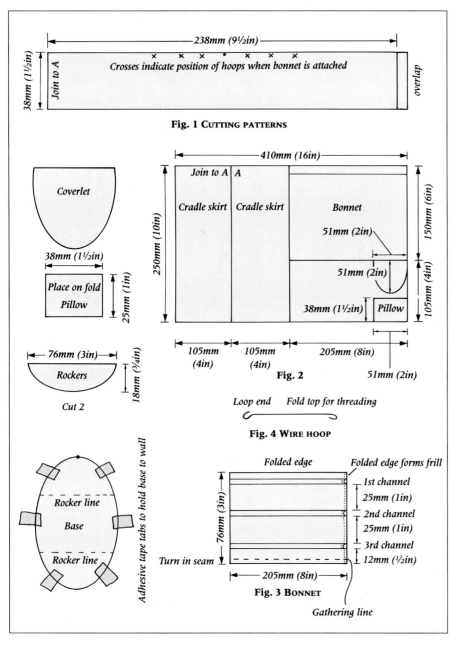

238mm (9½in)

38mm (1½in)

Join to A

Crosses indicate position of hoops when bonnet is attached

overlap

Fig. 1 CUTTING PATTERNS

Coverlet

38mm (1½in)

25mm (1in)

Place on fold
Pillow

410mm (16in)

Join to A | A

Cradle skirt | Cradle skirt

Bonnet

51mm (2in)

51mm (2in)

38mm (1½in) | Pillow

250mm (10in)

150mm (6in)

105mm (4in)

105mm
(4in)

105mm
(4in)

205mm (8in)

51mm (2in)

Fig. 2

76mm (3in)

Rockers

18mm (¾in)

Cut 2

Loop end   Fold top for threading

Fig. 4 WIRE HOOP

Rocker line

Base

Rocker line

Adhesive tape tabs to hold base to wall

Folded edge

Folded edge forms frill

76mm (3in)

1st channel
25mm (1in)

2nd channel
25mm (1in)

3rd channel
12mm (½in)

Turn in seam

205mm (8in)

Fig. 3 BONNET

Gathering line

You Will Need
~

- Card, approximately 250 × 130mm (10 × 5in)
- Lining silk, approximately 250 × 130mm (10 × 5in)
- 5mm (¼in) wadding, approximately 250 × 130mm (10 × 5in)
- White cotton, approximately 360 × 250mm (14 × 10in)
- Fabric adhesive
- Dress-making pins

- Ribbon to trim 460mm (18in)
- Milliner's wire or strong, fine wire 380mm (15in)
- Needle-nosed pliers
- Organdie, approximately 410 × 250mm (16 × 10in)
- Lace or braid to trim, 1m (39in)
- 6mm (¼in) balsa wood, 76mm × 18mm (3 × ¾in)
- White enamel paint (optional)
- Sealer (to seal balsa, optional)

1. Cut a template for the cradle base and wall and use it as a pattern for cutting out the silk lining, the wadding and the cotton outer covering, adding a 3mm (⅛in) turning allowance all round for the silk and cotton pieces.

2. Cut out the pieces in card and staple the foot of the cradle at the overlap. Align the dots on both pieces and glue the base to the body. You will find it easier if you place small pieces of adhesive tape under the base and use these to hold the side in place.

3. Glue a white cotton covering to the outside surface of the cradle, which will make it easier to sew the lining and bonnet to the cradle. Glue the wadding lightly in position inside the cradle.

4. Join the short ends of the silk cradle lining piece, then stitch it to the base. With the raw edges to the inside, drop it into position in the cradle. Fold the excess over the cradle rim and pin, then glue or sew in place.

5. Cut the bonnet pattern from the organdie. Fold the piece in half so that it measures approximately 205 × 76mm (8 × 3in). Sew the bottom edges – the 205mm (8in) edge – together; the dimensions given include a 3mm (⅛in) turning allowance. Turn to the right side and press flat. Turn in the raw edges at the open sides and catch down with small running stitches. Sew by hand or machine the three channels marked across the bonnet pieces (Fig. 3). Fasten off the ends. Use double thread to run a gathering line along the base of the piece, leaving the end sufficiently long to draw in later.

6. Cut three wire hoops, measuring 152, 127 and 105mm (6, 5 and 4in). Thread the longest through the first channel, bending the bottom of the wire to form a loop that will prevent the wire from slipping into the channel, and fold the top end tightly over to stop the point of the wire piercing or catching in the fabric. Use needle-nosed pliers to bend the wire. Thread the other two wires into the channels and adjust the gathers evenly. Gently arch the wires to form the bonnet shape. The finished length of the hoops should be 114, 89 and 64mm (4½, 3½ and 2½in). Snip off any excess and bend back the loops. Pull the gathering line at the back of the bonnet as tightly as possible and sew it to the

entry point to close up the back of the bonnet. Pin the bonnet in place on the body of the cradle, using a pin through each loop to hold it in place, then firmly sew it to the cradle.

7. Cut out the skirt strips and join them to measure 500 × 105mm (20 × 4in). Fold the fabric in half lengthways. Run two rows of gathering stitches along the top open edges, draw up the gathers and pin in place, matching up the centre with the dot on the cradle. Arrange and pin the gathers evenly around the cradle to meet at the centre back. Tie off the thread. Sew or glue in place. Trim to taste. The cradle illustrated here has two rows of an organdie edging around the cradle edge to cover the raw edges of the skirt gathers and bands of organdie edging sewn over the bonnet. A pink bow has been sewn at either side of the bonnet.

8. Cut out the coverlet pieces in organdie, lining silk and wadding, adding a 3mm (⅛in) turning allowance all round for the organdie and lining silk. Tack the wadding to the lining silk. Place the organdie on the lining side and sew around the edge, leaving the top open. Fasten off the thread and turn the right side out. Fold in the raw edges along the top and oversew neatly. Remove all tacking stitches. Trim with lace or edging.

9. Fold the pillow silk in half. Sew around the edges, leaving one side open. Turn the right side out, insert the wadding, sew the end edges together. Trim with lace or edging. Decorate the coverlet and pillow with bows if wished.

10. As an added extra, cut the rockers from balsa wood, seal with a proprietary sealer and paint with white matt enamel paint. Glue them to the cradle where indicated.

Screens

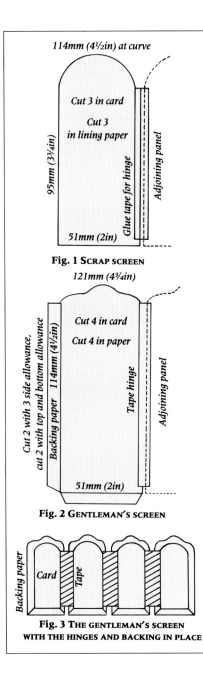

114mm (4½in) at curve

Cut 3 in card

Cut 3 in lining paper

95mm (3¾in)

Glue tape for hinge

Adjoining panel

51mm (2in)

Fig. 1 SCRAP SCREEN

121mm (4¾in)

Cut 4 in card

Cut 4 in paper

Cut 2 with 3 side allowance, cut 2 with top and bottom allowance

Backing paper 114mm (4½in)

Tape hinge

Adjoining panel

51mm (2in)

Fig. 2 GENTLEMAN'S SCREEN

Backing paper

Card

Tape

Fig. 3 THE GENTLEMAN'S SCREEN
WITH THE HINGES AND BACKING IN PLACE

You Will Need
~

- Approximately 125 × 205mm (5 × 8in) mounting card or similar
- Craft knife or scalpel
- 460mm (18in) cotton tape, 6mm (¼in) wide, or bias binding to match screen covering
- Strong paper glue
- Fine grade glass paper
- Satin varnish to finish

For Scrap Screen
- Lining or sugar paper
- Scrap design gift wrap paper suitable cut-out pictures and so on

For Gentleman's Screen
- Textured paper, mock lizard or book binding fabric
- 6mm (¼in) tape
- Small sets of hunting prints or suitable prints from magazines or gift wrapping paper

Making the Scrap Screen
1. Cut 3 panels in card.

2. Glue tape along one edge of two of the screen sections. The tape will act as a hinge.

3. Cut 3 panels in lining paper or sugar paper. Assemble the cut-out scraps and arrange them on each panel. When you have decided on the design, glue them to the panels, overlapping them to cover the backing paper completely.

4. Glue the decorated panels to the card panels. Press them firmly and smooth them with a dry, clean cloth. When the glue is dry, check that all the glued areas are stuck down.

5. Varnish the panels. Leave to dry for a few hours. Sand lightly with fine glass paper and apply a second coat of varnish. Repeat the sanding process and apply a third coat. If you wish, mix a drop of wood stain with the final coat of varnish to give an antique finish.

Making the Gentleman's Screen
1. Cut out the 4 panels in strong card. Cut 2 panels in textured paper, adding 3mm (⅛in) on three sides and two panels allowing 3mm (⅛in) at the top and bottom. Cut 4 panels of exact panel size for the front of the screen.

2. Glue 114mm (4½in) of tape down the outside edge of 3 of the 4 card panels to act as hinges.

3. Spread glue evenly over the paper panels and the extra allowances. Cover the card panels with paper.

4. The panels with the allowance at the top and bottom will be in the centre of the finished screen. Those with allowances on three edges will be at each end.

5. Join up the screen by gluing the tape to the adjoining panels. Glue the 4 front panels of paper to the front of the screen and decorate each panel with suitable prints, placing 3 or 4 on each panel. When they are firmly glued, varnish as for the scrap screen.

If the panels curl after decorating, sandwich between two boards and clamp, leaving overnight, to flatten.

THE DINING ROOM
~

Regency Dining Table

~

A beautiful reproduction table which will be the focus of any dining room. The construction of the legs – moulded column, leg holder and separate legs – is complex, but is much more elegant than the standard four-leg construction. You can of course simplify the moulding on the leg columns and leg holder.

~

MAKING THE TABLE TOP
~

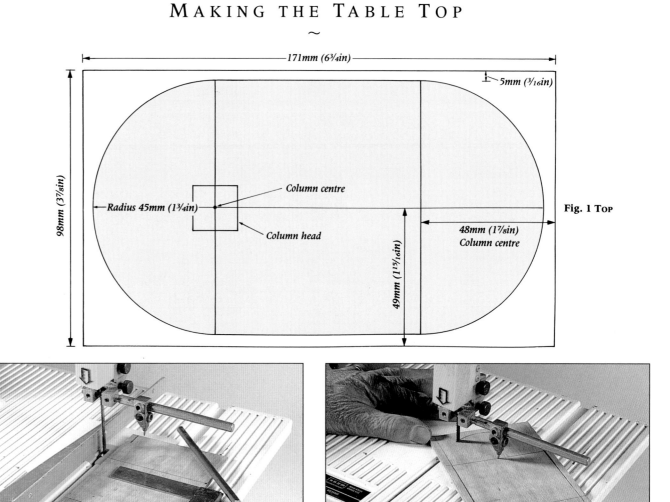

171mm (6¾in)

5mm (³⁄₁₆in)

98mm (3⅞in)

Radius 45mm (1¾in)

Column centre

Column head

48mm (1⅞in)
Column centre

49mm (1¹⁵⁄₁₆in)

Fig. 1 Top

1. Cut a rectangular blank 3mm (⅛in) thick to the measurements shown in Fig. 1. Mark on the shape of the table top and the horizontal and vertical lines; use a pencil so that you can rub out the lines when you have completed the table.

2. Cut out one of the straight edges, then a "D-end", then the second side and finally the other D-end.

MAKING THE LEG COLUMNS
~

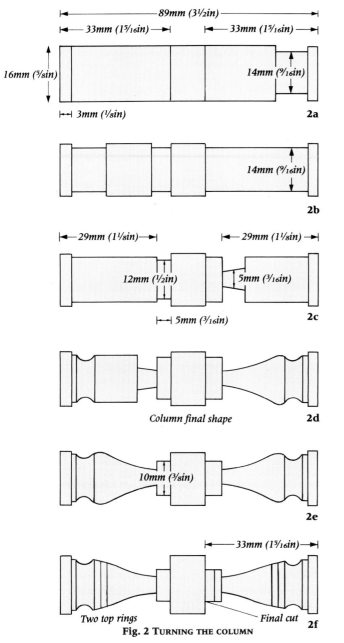

89mm (3½in)

33mm (1⁵/₁₆in)   33mm (1⁵/₁₆in)

16mm (⁵/₈in)

14mm (⁹/₁₆in)

3mm (¹/₈in)   **2a**

14mm (⁹/₁₆in)

2b

29mm (1¹/₈in)   29mm (1¹/₈in)

12mm (½in)   5mm (³/₁₆in)

5mm (³/₁₆in)   **2c**

Column final shape   **2d**

10mm (³/₈in)

2e

33mm (1⁵/₁₆in)

Two top rings   *Final cut*   **2f**
Fig. 2 TURNING THE COLUMN

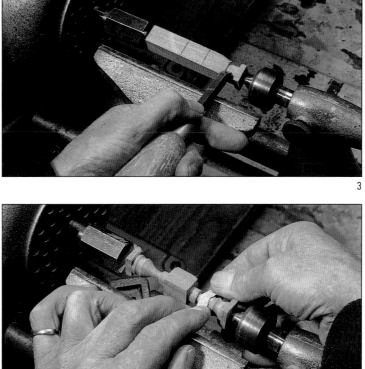

3

3. Cut a square-ended blank – one blank makes two columns – to the dimensions shown in Fig. 2a. The leg columns will then need to be shaped according to the sequence shown (Figs. 2b–e).

4

4. Hand sand the columns. Cut the two top rings (Fig. 2f). Cut the ring on the pad. Dust, stain and French polish the columns. Cut the columns to their final length – 33mm (1⁵/₁₆in).

5

5. Assemble the columns to the table top.

6. Dust, sand and polish the table top.

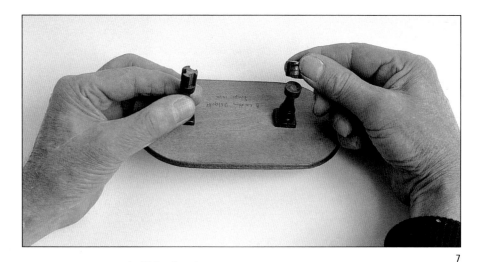

6

MAKING THE LEG HOLDERS

~

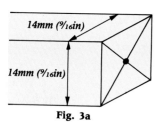

14mm (9/16in)

14mm (9/16in)

Fig. 3a

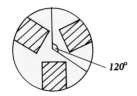

120°

Fig. 3d CUTTING SLOTS

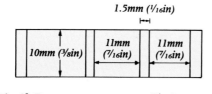

1.5mm (1/16in)

10mm (3/8in) | 11mm (7/16in) | 11mm (7/16in)

Fig. 3b BLANK TURNED TO 10MM (3/8IN) DIAMETER

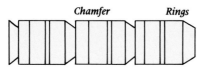

Chamfer   Rings

Fig. 3c RUNNING CHAMFER AND RINGS

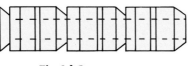

Fig. 3d CUTTING SLOTS

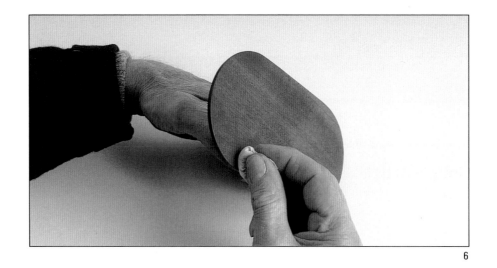

7

7. Cut a square-ended blank (Fig. 3a) and turn it so that it is 10mm (3/8in) in diameter (Fig. 3b). Cut rings and a chamfer (Fig. 3c). Stain and polish the pieces. Cut three slots down the sides of the piece at 120° to each other (Fig. 3d). Make the final cuts to give a length of 11mm (7/16in). Assemble the leg holders to the columns.

MAKING THE LEGS
~

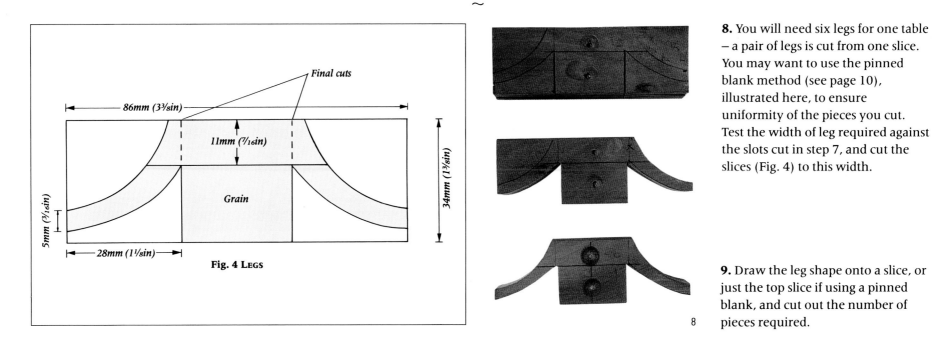

Final cuts

86mm (3³/₈in)

11mm (⁷/₁₆in)

34mm (1³/₈in)

5mm (³/₁₆in)

Grain

28mm (1¹/₈in)

Fig. 4 LEGS

8. You will need six legs for one table – a pair of legs is cut from one slice. You may want to use the pinned blank method (see page 10), illustrated here, to ensure uniformity of the pieces you cut. Test the width of leg required against the slots cut in step 7, and cut the slices (Fig. 4) to this width.

8

9. Draw the leg shape onto a slice, or just the top slice if using a pinned blank, and cut out the number of pieces required.

25mm (1in)

54mm (2¹/₈in)

48mm (1⁷/₈in)

60mm (2³/₈in)

48mm (1⁷/₈in)

89mm (3¹/₂in)

197mm (7³/₄in)

Fig. 5 FINAL ASSEMBLY JIG

9

10. Sand the top surfaces of the pieces, or pinned blank. Keep checking the finished height of the legs against the assembly jig (Fig. 5). Do not forget to tidy the underside of the legs. Using medium and fine sandpaper and working by hand, shape the surface. Stain and polish these surfaces.

11. Dismantle the pinned blank, if used, and check the height of the legs in the jig. Taper the legs with medium and fine sandpaper, stain and polish. Make the final cuts (Fig. 4) to the legs and fit the legs to the leg holders.

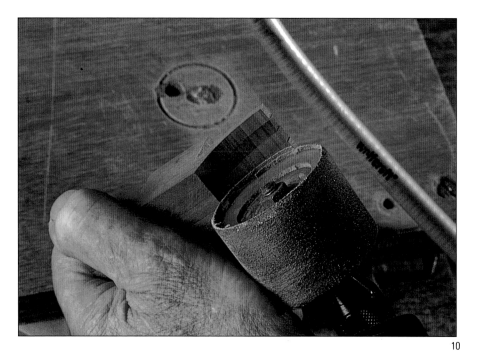

10

12. When you are satisfied with the height of the table, by checking against the jig, glue the legs in position in the leg holders and leave to dry overnight.

11

12

Chairs

~

Two delightful variations on the same design – a side chair and a carver for the head of the table – which complement the dining table design perfectly. To ensure that all four legs of your finished chairs touch the floor, choose sides that match as exactly as possible and use the special assembly jig described.

~

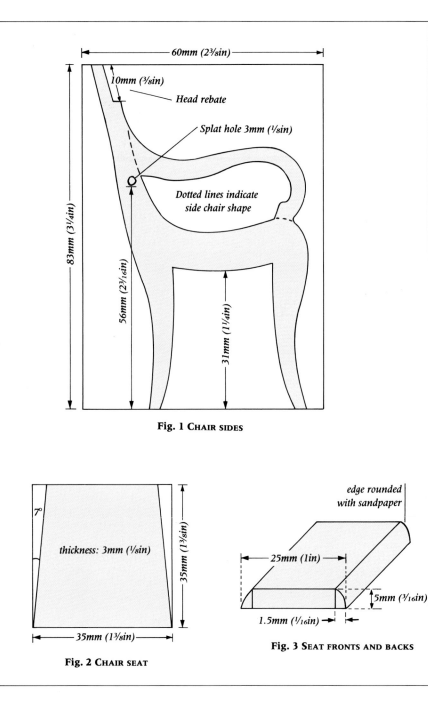

60mm (2⅜in)

10mm (⅜in)

Head rebate

Splat hole 3mm (⅛in)

Dotted lines indicate side chair shape

83mm (3¼in)

56mm (2³⁄₁₆in)

31mm (1¼in)

Fig. 1 CHAIR SIDES

7°

thickness: 3mm (⅛in)

35mm (1³⁄₈in)

35mm (1³⁄₈in)

Fig. 2 CHAIR SEAT

edge rounded with sandpaper

25mm (1in)

5mm (³⁄₁₆in)

1.5mm (¹⁄₁₆in)

Fig. 3 SEAT FRONTS AND BACKS

1

1. Cut slices for the chair sides to the measurements shown in Fig. 1. Make the slices 3mm (⅛in) wide. Belt or hand sand both sides of the slices. Draw the chair shapes on the slices. If you are making several chairs at once, use the pinned blank method (see page 10). Cut out the sides.

2

2. For the carver chair, you need to drill a hole in the centre of the arm as a point of entry for the saw. Finish cutting out the chair.

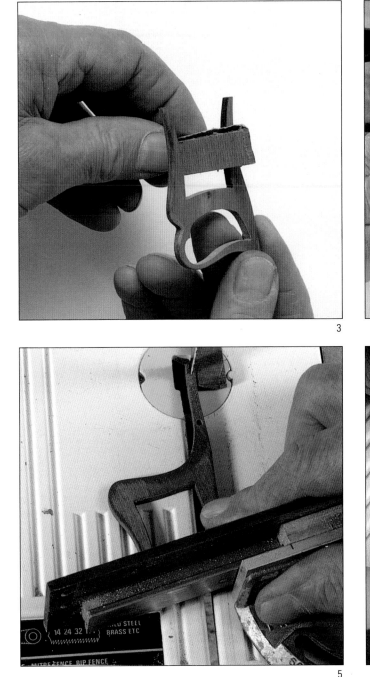

3

4

5

6

3. Sand all the surfaces. Keep the sides in matching pairs – mark this on the inside surface. Stain and polish all the surfaces which will show, including the underside of the carver arms. Slightly round the front edges of the sides with sandpaper.

4. Drill 3mm (1/8in) holes for the splats (decorative lateral pieces) as shown in Fig. 1.

5. Cut a rebate in the top of each side to hold the head (Fig. 1).

6. Cut the seat in pine (Fig. 2). Make the seat backs and fronts – cut a section 5mm (3/16in) wide and 25mm (1in) deep and the length of the seat. Hand sand both edges to give a rounded effect (Fig. 3). Stain and polish. Cut the fronts to 45mm (1¾in) and the backs to 31mm (1¼in). Glue to the seat and trim the ends. When the glue is dry, sand the edges of the seat so that the edgings are flush.

MAKING THE ASSEMBLY JIG
~

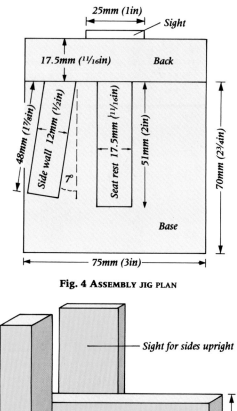

Fig. 4 ASSEMBLY JIG PLAN

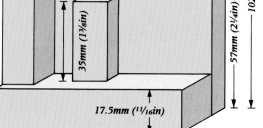

Fig. 4a ASSEMBLY JIG FRONT ELEVATION

Cut the base and mark the positions of the side wall and seat rest. Cut the back and pin and glue it to the base. Check that it is vertical with a small set square. Cut the side wall and seat rest pieces. Glue the side wall to the base and back. Check the vertical with a set square. Cut the "sight" piece and pin and glue it to the back. Check the vertical.

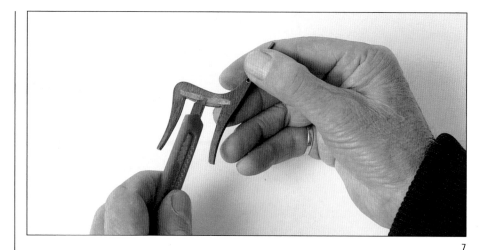

7

7. Scrape the inside area of the sides where they will be glued to the seat edges.

8. Place the left side of the chair flat against the side wall of the jig. Put glue on the left side of the seat. Place the seat on the seat rest and glue to the sides so that the front edge of the seat is 1.5mm (¹/₁₆in) in from the front of the side. When the glue has set, place the right side on the jig, lining it up with the jig sighter, but do not glue.

8

MAKING THE SPLAT
~

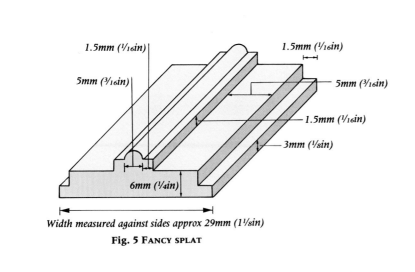

1.5mm (¹/₁₆in)

5mm (³/₁₆in)

1.5mm (¹/₁₆in)

5mm (³/₁₆in)

1.5mm (¹/₁₆in)

3mm (¹/₈in)

6mm (¹/₄in)

Width measured against sides approx 29mm (1¹/₈in)

Fig. 5 FANCY SPLAT

10

10. In this case, a whole section has been moulded to the shape of the splat, so thin sections have to be sliced off to a width of slightly more than 1.5mm (¹/₁₆in). Hand sand, stain and polish the back of the strips. Drill a 1.5mm (¹/₁₆in) hole in the centre of the splat for decoration.

9

9. Next, make the splat (Fig. 5). This can be straight or a more ornamented one as illustrated.

11

11. You may need to trim the ends of the splats to ensure a snug fit in the sides. Insert glue in the holes and assemble the splat to the left hand side on the jig. Place the right side on the jig and insert the other end of the splat in the hole. Check that all the legs are flat on the jig base.

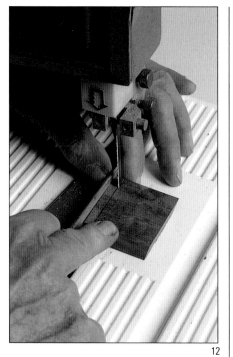

12. Cut the head to thickness of the rebate cut in the chair side (Fig. 6). Glue the head in position, making sure that the overhang at both ends is even.

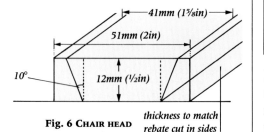

41mm (1⅝in)

51mm (2in)

10°   12mm (½in)

Fig. 6 CHAIR HEAD   *thickness to match rebate cut in sides*

MAKING THE UPHOLSTERED SEAT
~

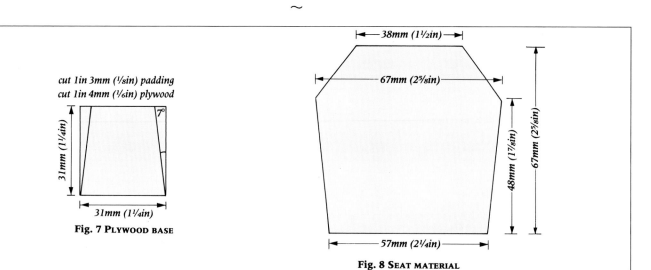

cut 1in 3mm (⅛in) padding
cut 1in 4mm (⅙in) plywood

31mm (1¼in)   7°

31mm (1¼in)

Fig. 7 PLYWOOD BASE

38mm (1½in)

67mm (2⅝in)

48mm (1⅞in)   67mm (2⅝in)

57mm (2¼in)

Fig. 8 SEAT MATERIAL

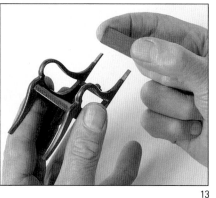

13. Cut a seat shape from 4mm (⅙in) plywood to the measurements in Fig. 7. Cut out a piece of foam or padding the same size. Glue the padding to the plywood. Cut out material using the pattern in Fig. 8. Cover the seat with the material and glue the edges in place. Glue onto the chair.

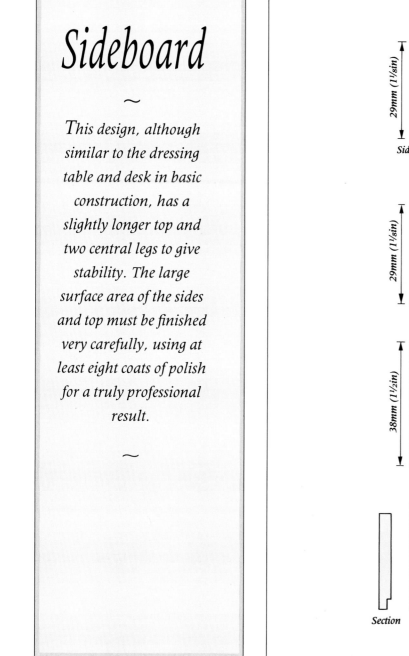

Sideboard

~

This design, although similar to the dressing table and desk in basic construction, has a slightly longer top and two central legs to give stability. The large surface area of the sides and top must be finished very carefully, using at least eight coats of polish for a truly professional result.

~

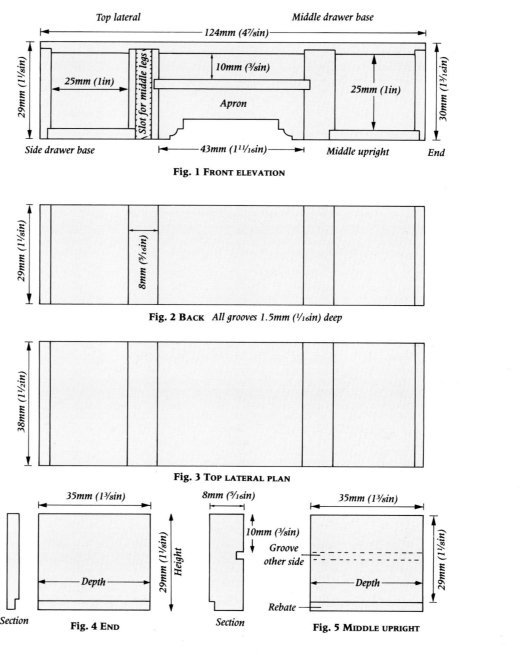

Top lateral   Middle drawer base

124mm (4⁷⁄₈in)

29mm (1⅛in)

25mm (1in)

Slot for middle legs

10mm (³⁄₈in)

Apron

25mm (1in)

30mm (1³⁄₁₆in)

Side drawer base   43mm (1¹¹⁄₁₆in)   Middle upright   End

Fig. 1 FRONT ELEVATION

29mm (1⅛in)

8mm (⁵⁄₁₆in)

Fig. 2 BACK *All grooves 1.5mm (¹⁄₁₆in) deep*

38mm (1½in)

Fig. 3 TOP LATERAL PLAN

35mm (1³⁄₈in)

8mm (⁵⁄₁₆in)

35mm (1³⁄₈in)

10mm (³⁄₈in)

Groove other side

29mm (1⅛in) Height

Depth

Section   **Fig. 4 END**

Section

Depth

Rebate

29mm (1⅛in)

Fig. 5 MIDDLE UPRIGHT

1. Cut the back from 4mm (⅙in) plywood. Cut the top lateral, from your chosen wood, to 3mm (⅛in) thick. Run grooves and rebates as shown in Figs. 2 and 3. All grooves should be 1.5mm (¹⁄₁₆in) deep.

2. Cut two middle uprights to the dimensions shown in Fig. 5. Run a 1.5mm (¹⁄₁₆in) groove to one side and a 3mm (⅛in) rebate on the other side. Cut two ends 3mm (⅛in) thick as shown in Fig. 4. Run a rebate in the ends.

3. Run slots 5mm (³⁄₁₆in) wide and 3mm (⅛in) deep in the middle uprights for the middle legs.

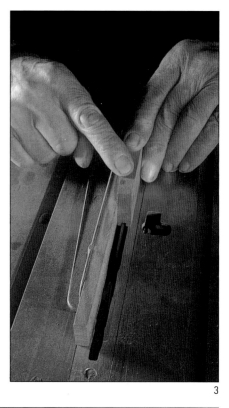

1

2

3

4. Assemble the back, top lateral and middle uprights of the carcass on a jig. Apply glue to the grooves on the back, the middle upright and the top edge. Glue the top of the lateral to the top edge of the back. Glue the middle uprights to the back and top lateral. Allow the glue to dry.

5. Apply glue to the rebates for the ends on the back and top lateral and glue the ends in place. Allow the glue to dry.

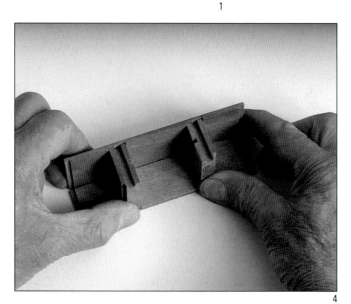

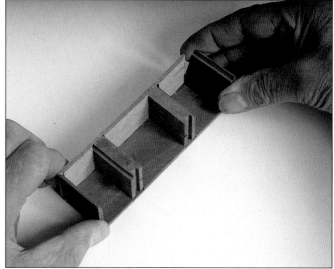

4

5

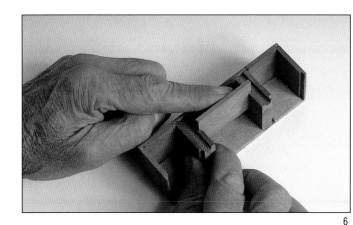

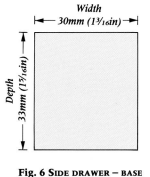

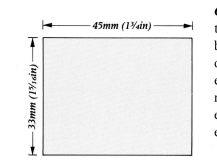

Fig. 6 SIDE DRAWER – BASE

Width 30mm (1³⁄₁₆in)
Depth 33mm (1⁵⁄₁₆in)

Fig. 7 MIDDLE DRAWER – BASE

45mm (1¾in)
33mm (1⁵⁄₁₆in)

6. Cut out one base 3mm (⅛in) thick for the middle drawer and two bases 3mm (⅛in) thick for the side drawers (Figs. 6 and 7). Sand the ends and bottom of the carcass on medium paper on a flat surface. The ends must be flush for gluing the end panels.

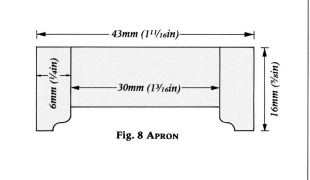

43mm (1¹¹⁄₁₆in)
6mm (¼in)
30mm (1³⁄₁₆in)
16mm (⅝in)

Fig. 8 APRON

7. Next cut the apron. You will need a rectangular block of wood for the central piece 30 × 10mm (1³⁄₁₆ × ³⁄₈in) and at least 38mm (1½in) long. Cut two pieces 16 × 6mm (⅝ × ¼in) for the side pieces to the same length; these will have to be shaped as shown (Fig. 8).

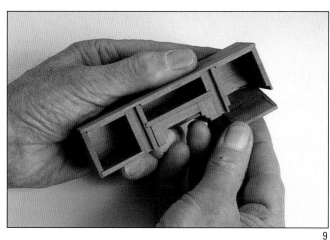

8. Glue the apron components together and slice off a piece 3mm (⅛in) thick.

9. Fit and glue the apron and drawer bases to the carcass. Sand the front of the carcass on a sheet of medium sandpaper on a flat surface so that all the front members are flush, dust off, stain and French polish.

MAKING THE LEGS
~

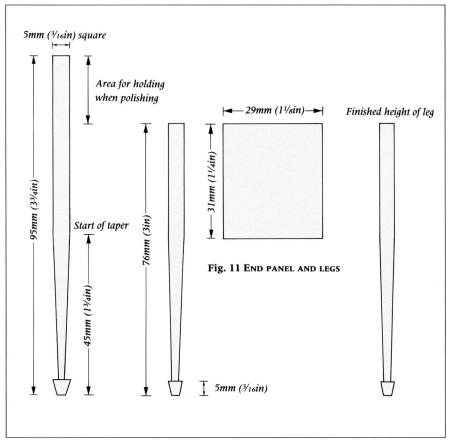

5mm (³/₁₆in) square

Area for holding when polishing

95mm (3¾in)

Start of taper

45mm (1¾in)

76mm (3in)

29mm (1⅛in)

31mm (1¼in)

Finished height of leg

5mm (³/₁₆in)

Fig. 11 END PANEL AND LEGS

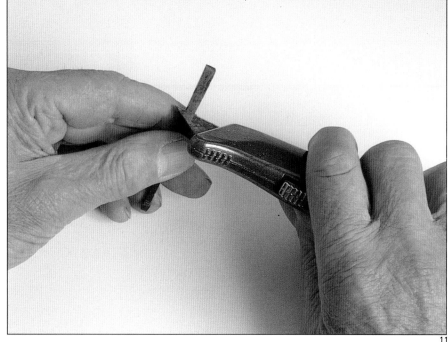

11

11. The inside of the legs and parts of the panels to be glued to the carcass should be scraped with a craft knife to remove all polish, otherwise the glue will not adhere.

12. Glue the middle legs to the carcass. Make sure all the legs touch the floor.

10. For the legs, you will need six square blanks. Taper the legs to the shape shown in Fig. 11. Fine sand, dust, stain and polish the legs. Cut the legs to the finished length. Cut two end panels 3mm (⅛in) thick. Sand, dust, stain and polish one side. Assemble the legs and end panels on a jig. Make sure the leg tops and the top of the panel align exactly.

10

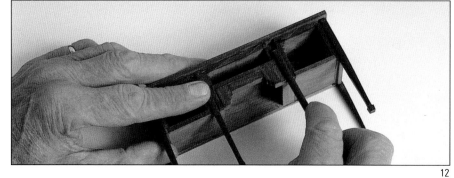

12

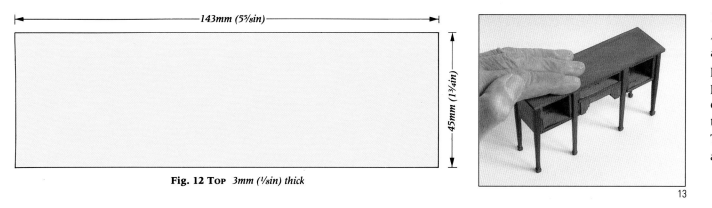

← 143mm (5⅝in) →

45mm (1¾in)

Fig. 12 Top *3mm (⅛in) thick*

13. Cut out the table top (Fig. 12). Apply glue to the top of the carcass and position the top. Test the end panels for fit. Remove the end panels. When the glue is completely dry, dust, stain and polish the table top. Glue the end panels in position. The back legs line up with the back and the front legs protrude slightly.

13

MAKING A SET OF DRAWERS
~

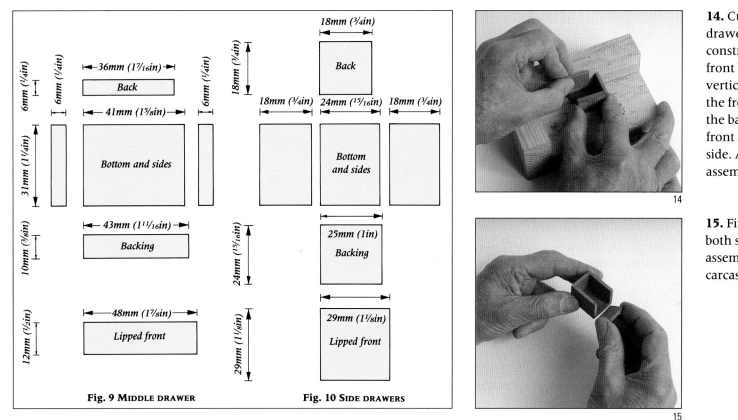

6mm (¼in)

6mm (¼in)

← 36mm (1⁷⁄₁₆in) →

Back

← 41mm (1⅝in) →

31mm (1¼in)

Bottom and sides

← 43mm (1¹¹⁄₁₆in) →

10mm (⅜in)

Backing

← 48mm (1⅞in) →

12mm (½in)

Lipped front

Fig. 9 MIDDLE DRAWER

18mm (¾in)

18mm (¾in)

Back

18mm (¾in) 24mm (¹⁵⁄₁₆in) 18mm (¾in)

18mm (¾in)

Bottom and sides

24mm (¹⁵⁄₁₆in)

25mm (1in)

Backing

29mm (1⅛in)

29mm (1⅛in)

Lipped front

Fig. 10 SIDE DRAWERS

14. Cut out components for two side drawers and one middle drawer. To construct a drawer, place the drawer front backing piece against the vertical back of the jig. Apply glue to the front of the drawer bottom and the backing piece. Apply glue to the front and bottom of the right-hand side. Allow the glue to dry and assemble the left side.

14

15. Fit the back by applying glue to both sides and bottom, and assemble. Fit the drawer to the carcass.

15

16. The lipped drawer front should overlap all the drawer edges by 1.5mm ($\frac{1}{16}$in). You can test this against a rebate 1–2mm ($\frac{1}{16}$in) deep run in a piece of scrap. Drill a hole in the centre of the drawers for the knobs and glue the knobs in place.

16

Fire Surround

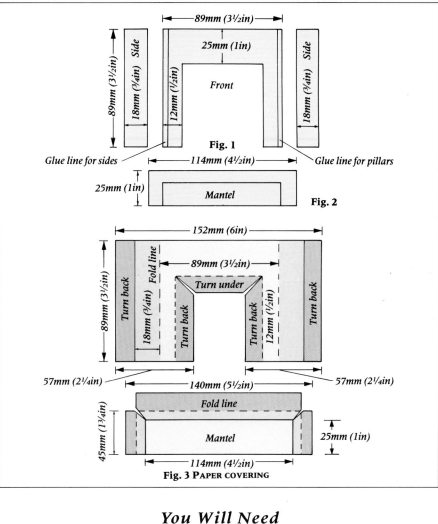

Fig. 1

Side — 89mm (3½in)

89mm (3½in)

18mm (¾in)

12mm (½in)

25mm (1in)

Front

Side

18mm (¾in)

Glue line for sides — 114mm (4½in) — Glue line for pillars

Fig. 2

25mm (1in)

Mantel

Fig. 3 PAPER COVERING

152mm (6in)

Turn back — Fold line

89mm (3½in)

89mm (3½in)

Turn under

18mm (¾in)

12mm (½in)

Turn back

Turn back

Turn back

Turn back

57mm (2¼in) — 140mm (5½in) — 57mm (2¼in)

Fold line

Mantel

45mm (1¾in)

25mm (1in)

114mm (4½in)

You Will Need
~

☞ Wood (pine, obeche or similar) for surround 89 × 127 × 3mm (3½ × 5 × ⅛in); for mantel 25 × 114 × 5mm (1 × 4½ × ³⁄₁₆in)

☞ 6mm (¼in) dowel, 2 pieces each 89mm (3½in)

☞ Marbled paper to cover wood

☞ Wood adhesive

1. Cut the wood pieces. Glue the side pieces to the back of the surround. When the glue is dry, stick marbled paper over the front and sides. Smooth the covering firmly with a clean, dry cloth.

2. Cover the mantelpiece with marbled paper and glue it firmly to the surround.

3. Cover the two pieces of dowel with paper; you will need about 25 × 89mm (1 × 3½in) of paper for each pillar. When the glue is dry, run a line of glue down each side of the surround as indicated on Fig. 1. Put a spot of glue on top of the pillars and press them into position, holding them in place until dry.

4. Your surround can now be glued into place in your doll's house or room setting. Glue a piece of contrasting marbled paper over a hearth stone made from a piece of card measuring approximately 114 × 51mm (4½ × 2in) to complement the finished surround.

French Metal Chandelier

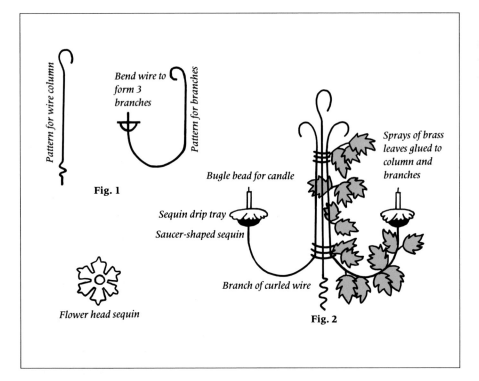

Pattern for wire column

Bend wire to form 3 branches

Pattern for branches

Fig. 1

Bugle bead for candle

Sequin drip tray

Saucer-shaped sequin

Sprays of brass leaves glued to column and branches

Branch of curled wire

Fig. 2

Flower head sequin

You Will Need
~

- Strong wire for branches, three pieces, each approximately 105mm (4in)
- Needlepoint pliers
- Strong wire for the column, 76mm (3in)
- Fine wire for lashings
- Superglue gel
- Brass foliage (available in sheets from good craft shops)
- Enamel gloss paint (2 shades of green)
- Tweezers
- 3 flower-shaped, mother-of-pearl sequins for candle drip trays
- 3 saucer-shaped sequins or brass jewellery findings
- 3 glass bugle beads for candles (available from craft or bead shops)
- 3mm (⅛in) ribbon, approximately 150mm (6in)

1. Bend the three branches into shape with needle-nosed pliers, using Fig. 1 as a guide. Bind these tightly to the column with fine wire, spacing them evenly around the column. Hang the skeleton from a craft stand or "third hand" and, after checking that the branches are correctly spaced, apply some glue to the lashings to hold the branches firm. Paint column and branches green.

2. Cut off a quarter of a sheet of leaves (ivy leaves were used here) and use two shades of green to paint the leaves to give the effect of light and shade. When the paint is dry, turn the sheet over and repeat on the other side.

3. When the paint is dry, cut the leaves free from the sheet and bend them into natural shapes. Glue sprays of leaves to the branches and column with superglue. Use tweezers to press them into position if necessary.

4. When the glue is set, thread the saucers onto the branches, making sure that they do not drop too far down. Hold them in position until the glue is set. Add a flower-head sequin to each branch, followed by a bugle bead. Snip off any excess wire and dab the tip of the wire with superglue to stop the beads from falling off.

5. Fold the ribbon in half and knot the ends together. Hang the chandelier from this ribbon, suspended from a ceiling hook in the doll's house.

Four-Branch Chandelier

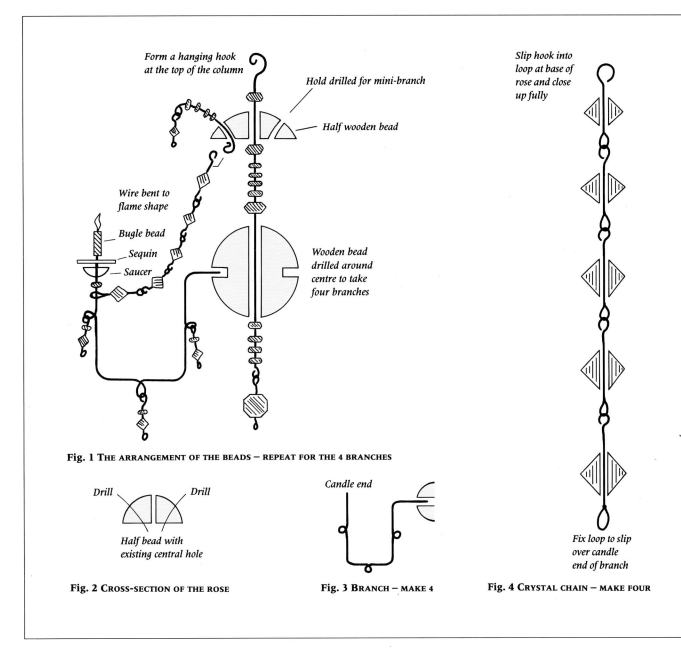

Form a hanging hook at the top of the column

Hold drilled for mini-branch

Half wooden bead

Wire bent to flame shape

Bugle bead

Sequin

Saucer

Wooden bead drilled around centre to take four branches

Slip hook into loop at base of rose and close up fully

Fig. 1 THE ARRANGEMENT OF THE BEADS – REPEAT FOR THE 4 BRANCHES

Drill   Drill

Half bead with existing central hole

Fig. 2 CROSS-SECTION OF THE ROSE

Candle end

Fig. 3 BRANCH – MAKE 4

Fix loop to slip over candle end of branch

Fig. 4 CRYSTAL CHAIN – MAKE FOUR

You Will Need
~

- 48 small, clear glass beads for the column and the 4 crystal-bearing mini-branches
- 4 fat-ended crystal cut beads for central column (the one at the bottom should be slightly larger)
- 20 facet-cut (crystal) beads for crystal chains
- 4 facet-cut (crystal) beads for mini-branches at rose level
- 12 facet-cut (crystal) beads for drops on main branches
- 4 sequins for drip trays
- 4 concave jewellery findings for base of drip trays (optional)
- Strong wire for column and branches
- Finer craft wire for chain links and to hook beads to each other
- 2 large wooden beads, 18mm (¾in), to make the rose and bulbous base
- Thick gold felt-tipped pen to colour beads
- Spiral drill for drilling holes through the rose and ball base to take the wire branches
- Small saw for cutting the wooden beads in half
- Needle-nosed pliers for bending wires to shape and cutting to required length
- Tweezers to nip chain link ends together.

1. Cut one of the large wooden beads in half. Drill four holes diagonally through the domed shape at equal intervals (Fig. 2). Colour this with the gold pen. This is the rose.

2. Pass a 31mm (1¼in) length of wire through each hole and bend the bottom end of each wire emerging from the flat undersurface of the bead into a closed loop (Fig.1). In Fig. 1 each bead is shown widely spaced for clarity. On the end of each branch emerging from the curved top surface, thread four small, clear glass beads. Bend the wire into a closed loop, snipping off any excess with pliers. Thread one crystal bead onto fine wire, make a small loop at one end to keep the bead on, bend the other end into a hook, snipping off the excess, then hang the crystal drop from the loop on the mini-branch. Repeat for the other three branches.

3. Cut strong wire to form a column 64mm (2½in) long. Bend the top into a hanging hook, then thread on one flat-ended crystal, the half wooden rose bead, one flat-ended crystal bead, four plain, clear glass and one flat-ended crystal bead.

4. Before continuing, drill four holes horizontally through the second wooden bead, spacing them evenly around the bead (Fig. 1), and colour

it gold. Use the existing hole to thread this on the column and then add four clear glass beads. Form the wire into a closed loop and trim off the excess. Then thread one large crystal bead onto a short wire, forming a short loop to keep the bead on the wire. Bend the wire at the other end into a hook and hang from the loop on the column.

5. Make four wire branches using the outline in Fig. 3 as a guide for size and shape. Using superglue to glue each branch firmly into the four drilled holes in the round bead. You will find it easier to work if you hang the chandelier from a craft stand. Thread drops of one plain bead and one crystal on thin wire and hang them from the three loops formed on each of the four branches (this will take 12 such drops). Make four chains of finer wire with five crystal beads each (Fig. 4). Nip in the ends of the loops well to secure. Hook one end of each chain to the loops on the underside of the rose and nip shut, slip the loops over the candle-bearing ends of the branches.

6. When all the chains are in place, thread a saucer (optional) and sequin over each branch, topping each with a bugle bead. Bend the excess wire to form a flame and snip off the excess. For extra length, hang the chandelier on a ribbon or chain from the ceiling hook.

THE LIVING ROOM
~

Bookshelves

~

These pretty shelves have a similar side design to the hanging shelves, but the use of a mahogany-style wood gives the piece a more substantial, old-fashioned look suitable for a drawing room. Since the back is visible and decorative, it needs to have the same level of finish as the sides and shelves; it can be made either with solid mahogany or with a mixture of plywood-backed veneer and mahogany.

~

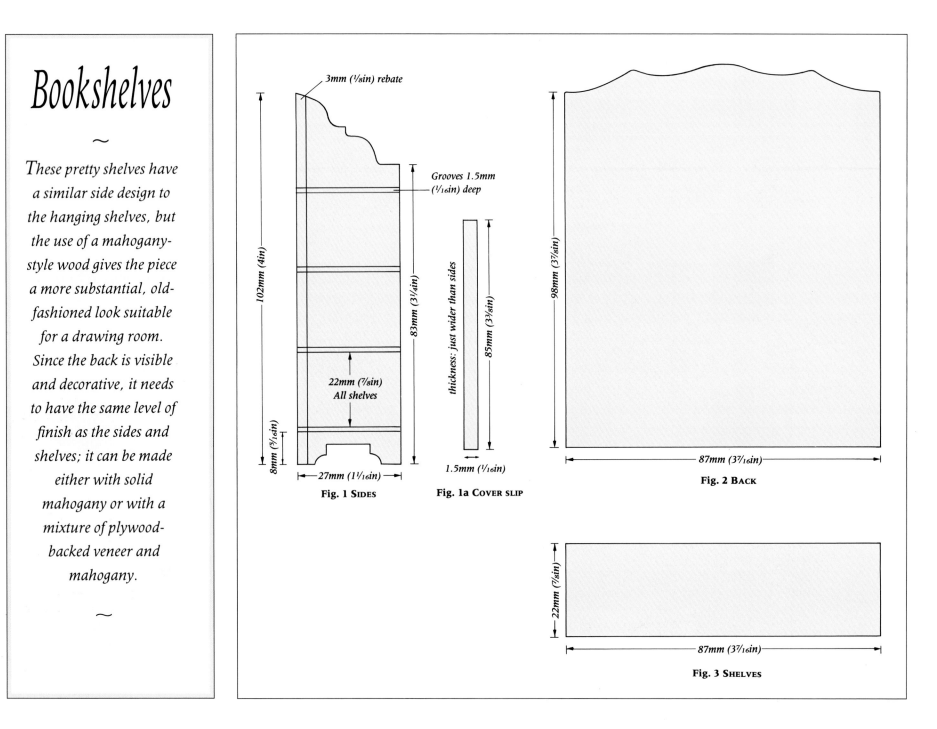

3mm (⅛in) rebate

Grooves 1.5mm (¹⁄₁₆in) deep

102mm (4in)

83mm (3¼in)

22mm (⅞in) All shelves

8mm (⁵⁄₁₆in)

27mm (1¹⁄₁₆in)

Fig. 1 SIDES

thickness: just wider than sides

85mm (3⅜in)

1.5mm (¹⁄₁₆in)

Fig. 1a COVER SLIP

98mm (3⁷⁄₈in)

87mm (3⁷⁄₁₆in)

Fig. 2 BACK

22mm (⅞in)

87mm (3⁷⁄₁₆in)

Fig. 3 SHELVES

1

2

3

4

5

1. Cut slices for the sides measuring 25 × 114mm (1 × 4½in) and 3mm (⅛in) thick. Mark whether the side is an inside left or inside right. Draw on the shape of the sides in pencil (Fig. 1).

2. Run shelf grooves and rebates. Cut two cover slips (Fig. 1a) and glue them to the front edges of the sides. Sand the edges so the slips are flush with the outside surface of the blanks. Stain and polish the inside surface of the blank. Cut out the sides. You may wish to use the pinned blank method (page 10) if you are using power tools.

3. Two polished sides with the grooves and rebates ready cut. Cut the shelves to a thickness to match the grooves in the sides (Fig. 3). Stain and polish one surface and the front edge of the shelves. Stain, but do not polish, the underside of the shelves.

4. Cut out a blank for the back to a thickness of 3mm (⅛in) (Fig. 2). Mark the head shape in pencil. Stain and polish the surface.

5. Cut the head shape. Sand, stain and polish the top of the head shape. Insert glue into the grooves and both rebates on the sides.

Alternative Methods
~

87mm (3⁷/₁₆in)

122mm (4¹³/₁₆in)

98mm (3⁷/₈in)

Grain of veneer

83mm (3¹/₄in)

40mm (1⁹/₁₆in)

2mm (³/₃₂in) mahogany

1mm (¹/₃₂in) veneer

2mm (³/₃₂in) plywood

Fig. 4 ALTERNATIVE METHOD FOR BACK

Section Plan

6

6. Place the right side on the jig with the feet against the adjacent jig wall. Place the back on the jig to engage the back rebate. Position the back so that the top of the side-shaped head and the top of the back head align.

If you are using power tools, you may find it difficult to cut the head shape due to the thinness of the wood. Instead, you can use a combination of plywood and your chosen wood covered with a veneer. The head shape is cut in the good-quality wood, so that the top edge can be finished properly. Glue the two sections of wood together to form one sheet and glue on the veneer, with the grain running across the width. Hand sand and dust. Mark the head shape and stain and polish the veneered surface to about 6mm (¼in) beyond the outline of the head shape. Leave to dry. Cut the head shape.

7

7. Insert the shelves so that they are at right angles to one side. Add the left side, engaging the bottom shelf first and working upwards. Leave the glue to dry. Fine sand, stain and polish the outside surfaces of the sides.

Desk

~

The desk is smaller and squarer than both the sideboard and the dressing table but it is very similar in design. The main difference is the use of moulded strips of wood – "upstands" – to decorate the top surface; these strips are inserted into grooves on three sides of the top and give the piece a distinctive appearance.

~

All pieces 3mm (⅛in) thick unless otherwise stated

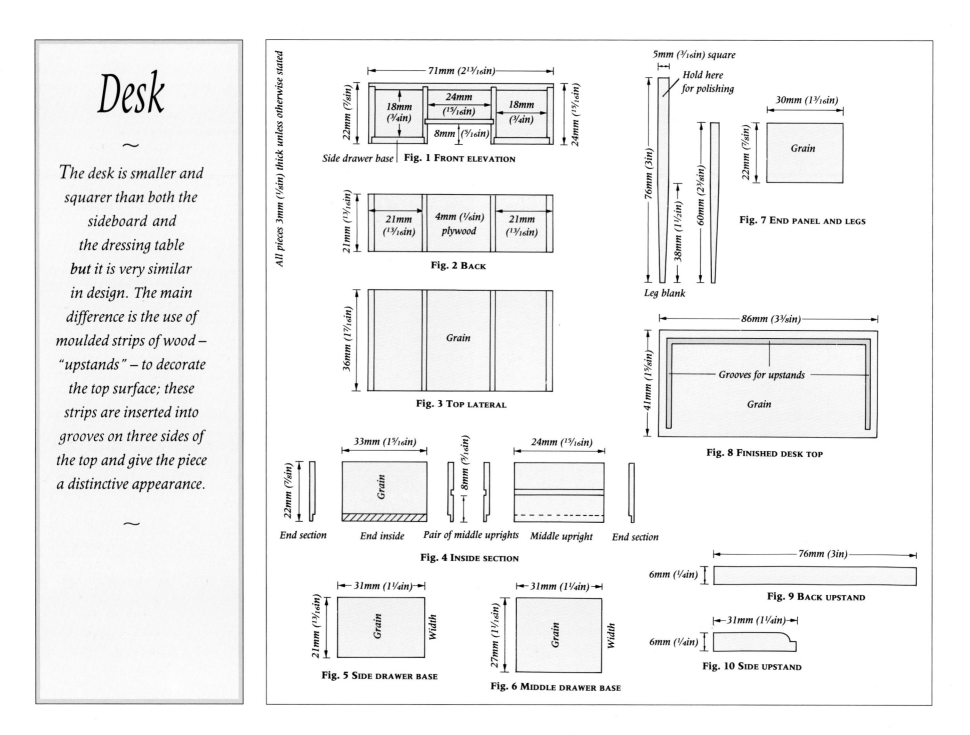

Fig. 1 FRONT ELEVATION

71mm (2¹³⁄₁₆in)

22mm (⅞in)

18mm (¾in)

24mm (¹⁵⁄₁₆in)

18mm (¾in)

24mm (¹⁵⁄₁₆in)

8mm (⁵⁄₁₆in)

Side drawer base

Fig. 2 BACK

21mm (¹³⁄₁₆in)

21mm (¹³⁄₁₆in)

4mm (⅙in) plywood

21mm (¹³⁄₁₆in)

Fig. 3 TOP LATERAL

36mm (1⁷⁄₈in)

Grain

Fig. 4 INSIDE SECTION

End section

22mm (⅞in)

33mm (1⁵⁄₁₆in)

Grain

End inside

8mm (⁵⁄₁₆in)

Pair of middle uprights

24mm (¹⁵⁄₁₆in)

Middle upright

End section

Fig. 5 SIDE DRAWER BASE

31mm (1¼in)

21mm (¹³⁄₁₆in)

Grain

Width

Fig. 6 MIDDLE DRAWER BASE

31mm (1¼in)

27mm (1¹⁄₁₆in)

Grain

Width

Fig. 7 END PANEL AND LEGS

5mm (³⁄₁₆in) square

Hold here for polishing

76mm (3in)

38mm (1½in)

60mm (2³⁄₈in)

Leg blank

30mm (1³⁄₁₆in)

22mm (⅞in)

Grain

Fig. 8 FINISHED DESK TOP

86mm (3³⁄₈in)

41mm (1⅝in)

Grooves for upstands

Grain

Fig. 9 BACK UPSTAND

76mm (3in)

6mm (¼in)

Fig. 10 SIDE UPSTAND

31mm (1¼in)

6mm (¼in)

1. Cut out the back from 4mm (⅙in) plywood. Cut the top lateral, the side drawer bases, the carcass ends, the middle uprights and the end panels all to a thickness of 3mm (⅛in); cut the middle drawer base to a thickness of 1.5mm (¹⁄₁₆in). Run 1.5mm (¹⁄₁₆in) grooves and rebates in all these pieces as indicated. Glue the back, top lateral and middle uprights in place. Sand all the edges flush. Glue the ends in place.

2. Sand, stain and polish the front of the carcass. Assemble the bases for all the drawers. Make four square-ended blanks for the legs. Use medium sandpaper to taper the legs, starting at the point indicated on Fig. 7. Sand, stain and polish the legs. Cut the legs to their final length.

3. Assemble the legs and end panels on a jig. Scrape away the polish from any surfaces to be glued. Make sure the leg tops and the top of the panel are exactly aligned.

4. Cut the top (Fig. 8) to 3mm (⅛in). Cut 1.5mm (¹⁄₁₆in) grooves 5mm (³⁄₁₆in) away from the back and side edges of the desk top for the "upstands". Position, but do not glue, the assembled end panels to the carcass. Glue the top in position.

5. Cut two strips 6 × 89mm (¼ × 3½in) and the thickness of the grooves in the top (Fig. 9). These will form the upstands to go around the edge of the top.

6. Polish one strip for the back upstand, holding one end. Hold the second strip in the middle and polish both ends. Leave the polish to harden overnight.

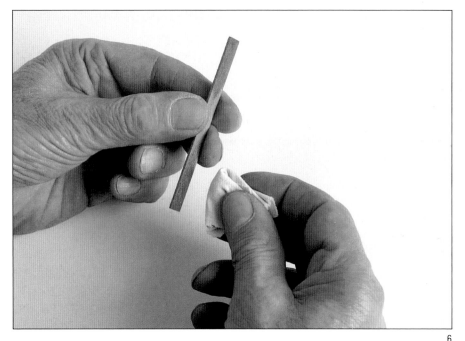

5

6

7. Cut the second upstand strip to form two 31mm (1¼in) lengths. Test the strips against the side grooves and cut if necessary. Mould the front ends of the side upstand pieces (Fig. 10). Sand and stain the moulding and retouch the polish.

8. To cut two end stops for the front of the desk, cut a section 25 × 11 × 11mm (1 × ⁷⁄₁₆ × ⁷⁄₁₆in) and slice it to the width of the grooves in the top. Cut a strip slightly wider than the depth of the grooves, and along the grain. Now cut four stops from the leftover strip for the other ends of the grooves; these need to be the width of the grooves and 5mm (³⁄₁₆in) long.

7

8

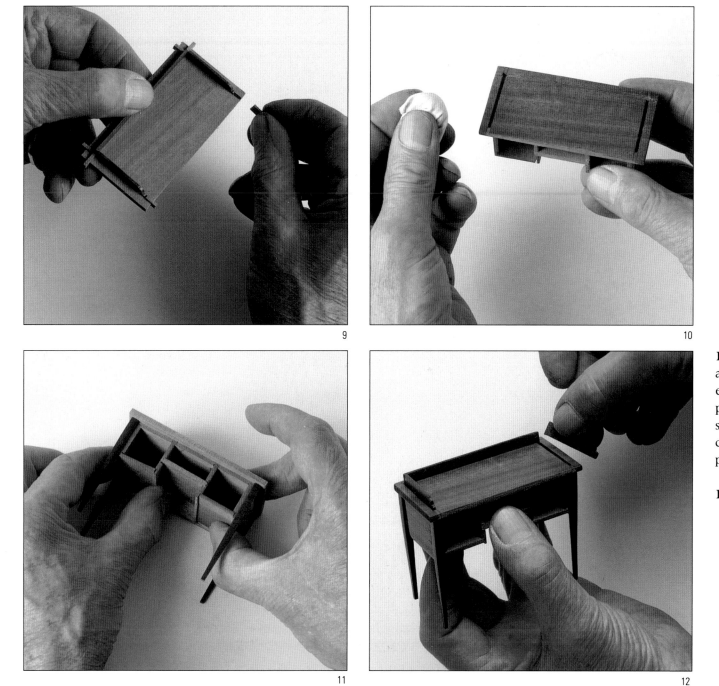

9

10

11

12

9. Dry-assemble the upstands to the desk top. Insert glue in the grooves for the stops and position them against the ends of the upstands. Wait for the glue to harden and remove the upstands. Trim and sand the ends of the stops.

10. Sand, stain and polish the top.

11. Check the alignment of the top and carcass against the assembled end panels and legs. Glue the end panels in position. The back legs should line up with the back of the carcass, the front legs should protrude slightly.

12. Glue the upstands in position.

M A K I N G   A   S E T   O F   D R A W E R S
~

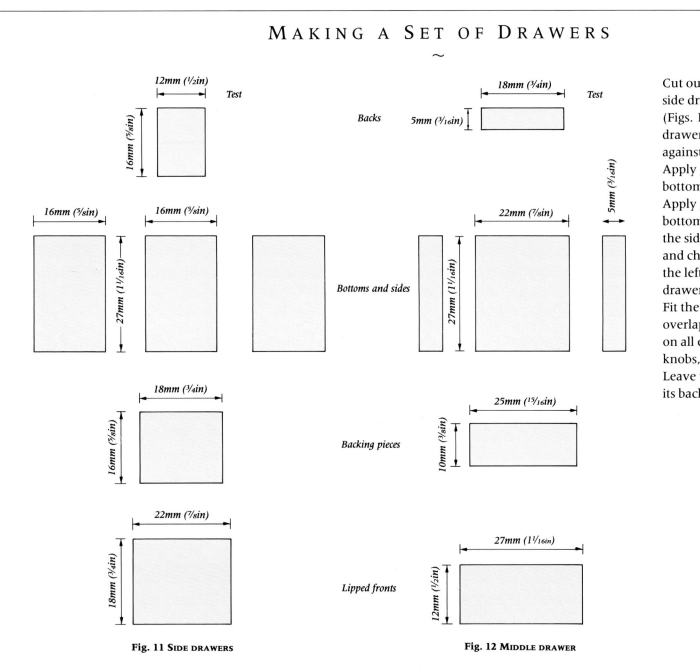

12mm (½in)
Test

16mm (⅝in)

Backs

18mm (¾in)
Test

5mm (³⁄₁₆in)

16mm (⅝in)

16mm (⅝in)

Bottoms and sides

22mm (⅞in)

5mm (³⁄₁₆in)

27mm (1¹⁄₁₆in)

27mm (1¹⁄₁₆in)

18mm (¾in)

Backing pieces

25mm (¹⁵⁄₁₆in)

16mm (⅝in)

10mm (³⁄₈in)

22mm (⅞in)

Lipped fronts

27mm (1¹⁄₁₆in)

18mm (¾in)

12mm (½in)

Fig. 11 SIDE DRAWERS

Fig. 12 MIDDLE DRAWER

Cut out drawer components for two side drawers and one middle drawer (Figs. 11 and 12). Assemble the drawers by placing the drawer front against the back of an assembly jig. Apply glue to the front of the drawer bottom and to the backing piece. Apply glue to the front and the bottom of the right-hand side. Push the side against the backing piece and check the alignment. Assemble the left side in the same way. Fit the drawers to the carcass. Fit the back. Fit the lipped fronts, which should overlap the fronts by 1.5mm (¹⁄₁₆in) on all edges. Drill holes for the knobs, apply glue and insert knobs. Leave the sideboard to dry on its back.

Occasional Table

~

This small table uses exactly the same construction as the Regency dining table, but it has a round top and needs only one leg, which is smaller than those on the dining table. The elegant design makes the table a splendid addition to any formal drawing room.

~

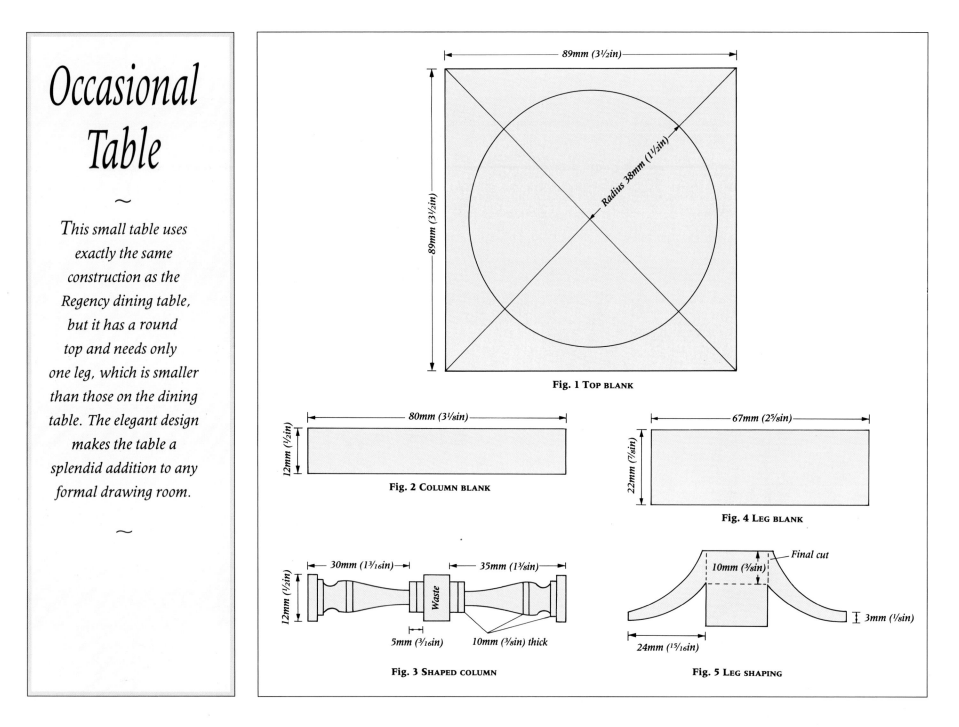

Fig. 1 TOP BLANK

Fig. 2 COLUMN BLANK

Fig. 4 LEG BLANK

Fig. 3 SHAPED COLUMN

Fig. 5 LEG SHAPING

1. Cut the circular table top to a radius of 38mm (1½in) from a blank 3mm (⅛in) thick. These four photographs show the stages of cutting the table top on a bandsaw using a circle cutting pin.

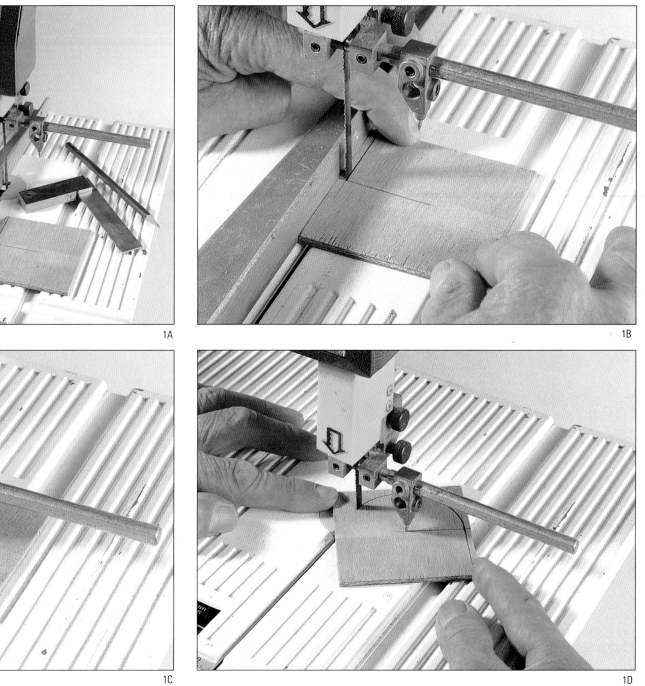

1A

1B

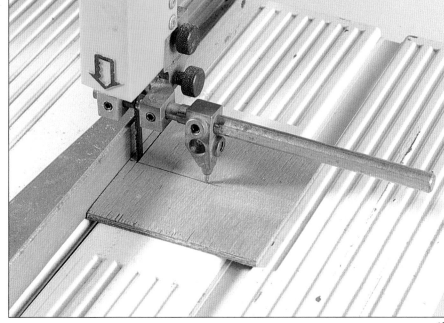

1C

1D

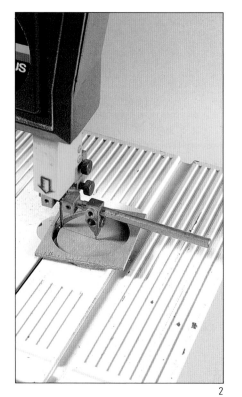

2

2. Completing the circle cut.

3. The cut table top and blocks for mounting it on the lathe.

4. Chamfer the edge of the table top. You can use a lathe if you have one, or simply sand the underside of the top. Finish by hand with medium and fine sandpaper.

5. The column, leg holder and legs are made in the same way as for the Regency Dining Table; the only difference is that this column is shorter.

4

3

5

MAKING THE COLUMNS
~

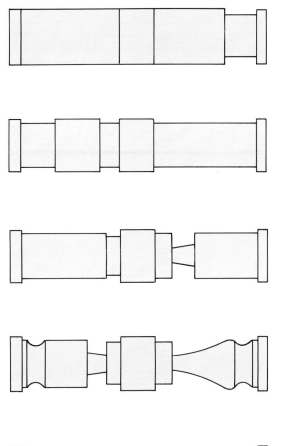

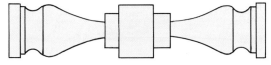

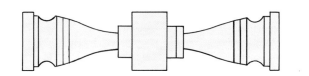

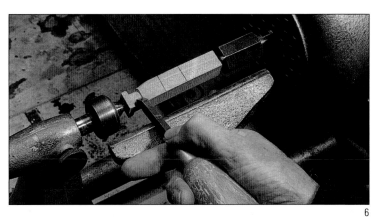

6

6. Cut a square-ended blank – one blank makes two columns – to the dimensions shown in Fig. 2. The leg column will then need to be shaped according to the sequence shown but ending up with a column to the dimensions shown in Fig. 3.

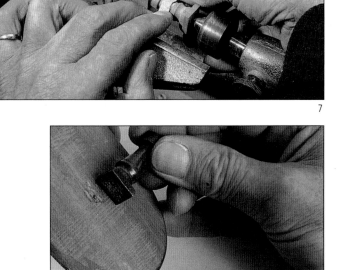

7

7. Hand-sand the column. Cut the two top rings. Cut the ring on the pad. Dust, stain and French polish the column. Cut the column to its final length – 30mm (1³⁄₁₆in).

8

8. Glue the column to the centre of the table top.

9. Dust, sand and polish the table top.

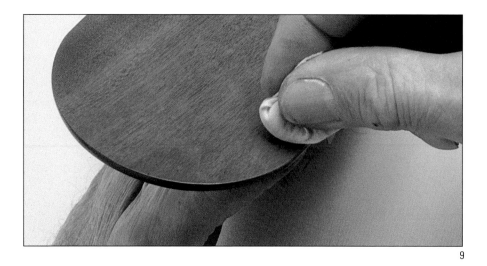

9

MAKING THE LEG HOLDERS
~

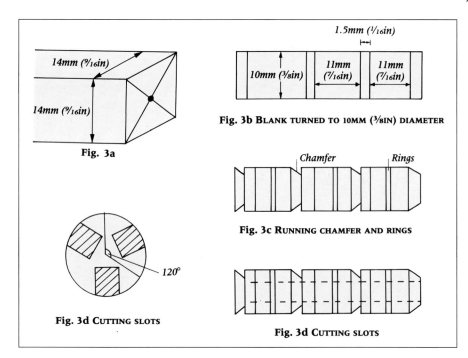

14mm (⁹⁄₁₆in)

14mm (⁹⁄₁₆in)

Fig. 3a

1.5mm (¹⁄₁₆in)

10mm (³⁄₈in)   11mm (⁷⁄₁₆in)   11mm (⁷⁄₁₆in)

Fig. 3b BLANK TURNED TO 10MM (³⁄₈IN) DIAMETER

Chamfer   Rings

Fig. 3c RUNNING CHAMFER AND RINGS

120°

Fig. 3d CUTTING SLOTS

Fig. 3d CUTTING SLOTS

10

10. For the leg holder, cut a square-ended blank (Fig. 3a) and turn it so that it is 10mm (³⁄₈in) in diameter (Fig. 3b). Cut rings and a chamfer (Fig. 3c). Stain and polish the pieces.

Cut three slots down the sides of the piece at 120° to each other (Fig. 3d). Make the final cuts to give a length of 11mm (⁷⁄₁₆in). Assemble the leg holders to the columns.

11

11. You will need three legs for one table – a pair of legs is cut from one slice. You may want to use the pinned blank method (see page 10), illustrated here, to ensure uniformity of the pieces you cut. Test the width of leg required against the slots cut in step 9, and cut the slices (Fig. 4) to this width. Glue the leg holder to the column. Draw the leg shape onto a slice, or just the top slice if using pinned blank, and cut out the number of pieces required.

12. Sand the legs and attach them to the leg holders. The final assembly jig is, in principle, the same as for the Regency Dining Table, except that there is space for only one column and the height from the floor of the jig to the top surface is 35mm (1⅜in). Place the table in the assembly jig and leave the glue to dry.

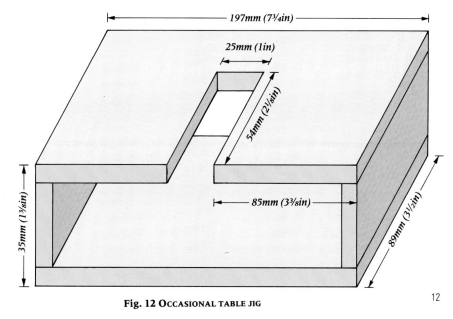

Fig. 12 OCCASIONAL TABLE JIG

12

The Occasional Table

Chesterfield Sofa

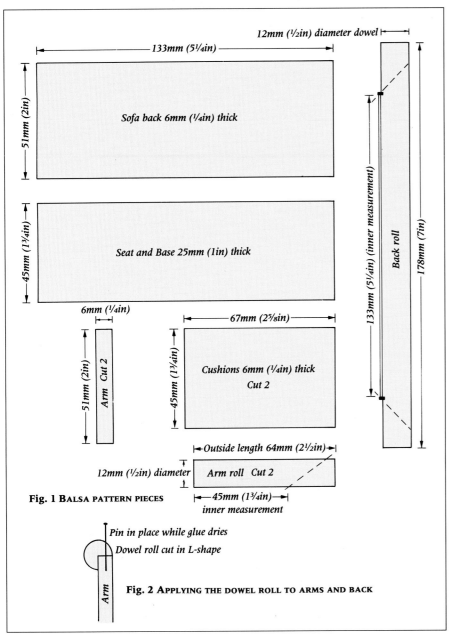

133mm (5¼in)

12mm (½in) diameter dowel

51mm (2in)

Sofa back 6mm (¼in) thick

45mm (1¾in)

Seat and Base 25mm (1in) thick

6mm (¼in)

67mm (2⅝in)

51mm (2in)

Arm Cut 2

45mm (1¾in)

Cushions 6mm (¼in) thick
Cut 2

133mm (5¼in) (inner measurement)

Back roll

178mm (7in)

Outside length 64mm (2½in)

12mm (½in) diameter

Arm roll Cut 2

Fig. 1 BALSA PATTERN PIECES

45mm (1¾in)
inner measurement

Pin in place while glue dries
Dowel roll cut in L-shape

Arm

Fig. 2 APPLYING THE DOWEL ROLL TO ARMS AND BACK

You Will Need
~

- Balsa wood for base 133 × 45 × 25mm (5¼ × 1¾ × 1in); for back 133 × 51 × 6mm (5¼ × 2 × ¼in); for arms (cut 2) 51 × 51 × 6mm (2 × 2 × ¼in); for cushions (cut 2) 67 × 45 × 6mm (2⅝ × 1¾ × ¼in)
- Sandpaper
- 380mm (15in) dowel 12mm (½in) in diameter
- Craft knife or scalpel
- Wood glue
- 25mm (1in) dress-making pins
- Wadding, approximately 205 × 205mm (8 × 8in)
- Fabric for covering (lightweight wool, cotton or silk), approximately 230mm (9in)
- Sewing thread
- Clear, all-purpose fabric adhesive
- 2 round-headed upholstery pins, 3mm (⅛in) in diameter, for ends of arms
- Hard wood, 25 × 25 × 3mm (1 × 1 × ⅛in), cut into 4 squares for feet

1. Cut out the balsa pieces. Smooth all the pieces with a sanding block. Sand the top edges of the two cushion pieces, rounding off the corners and shaving away a fraction on each edge so that they will fit onto the upholstered seat.

2. Cut the balsa dowel with the aid of a mitre block into two arm rolls, each 64mm (2½in) at the outer edge, and one back roll, 178mm (7in) at the outer edge. If you do not have a mitre block, draw a right angle with a set square on a wood-working board, divide the angle into 45° with a strong pencil line and use this as a guide for your cutting angle. Use a craft knife or scalpel to cut an L-shape out of the length of each piece of dowel (see Fig. 2).

3. Cut out the fabric pieces for the base (cut one), the back (cut one) and the arm pieces (cut two). Do not cut out the wadding at this stage. Glue the fabric for the sofa seat and front of base into position, starting at the back edge of the balsa base. When the back edge is secure, smooth the fabric forwards and down over the seat and glue it under the base. Glue both arm covers to the arms, and then glue back in the same way. Note that the fabric covers the outside surface, not the seat side, of the back. When the fabric covering is in position, glue the back of the sofa to the seat with wood glue. Clamp the pieces together until the glue is dry. Glue the arms in position. You can stick dress-making pins through the arms into the base to hold the arms.

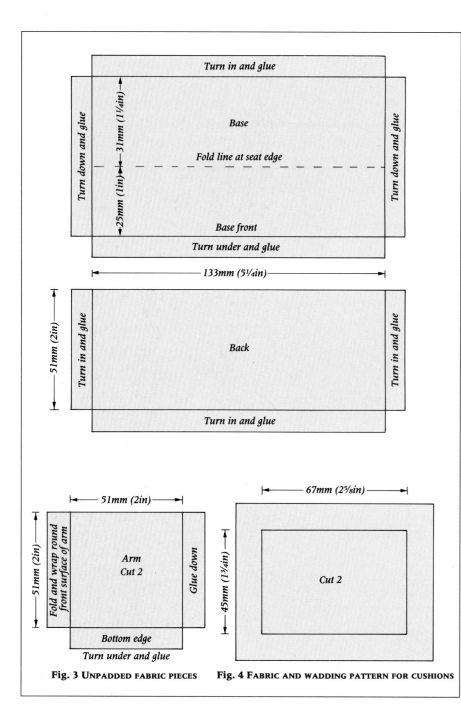

Fig. 3 UNPADDED FABRIC PIECES **Fig. 4 FABRIC AND WADDING PATTERN FOR CUSHIONS**

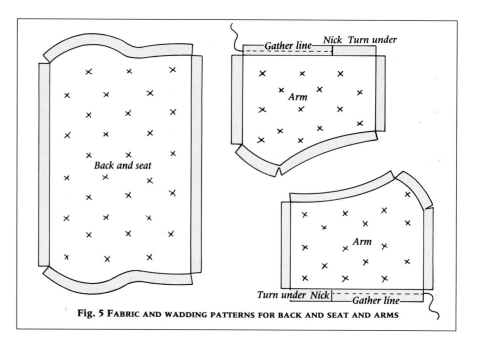

Fig. 5 FABRIC AND WADDING PATTERNS FOR BACK AND SEAT AND ARMS

4. Glue the rolls to the carcass. If the mitre ends do not fit, sand any excess or fill the gaps with a small piece of glue-soaked wadding.

5. For the buttoned-effect version, cut out the wadding and fabric pieces as shown in Figs. 4 and 5. Cut two cushion covers and two wadding pieces. Note that the wadding for the cushions should be cut exactly to size, with no allowance for edging. Draw the dots on the wadding for the arms and back. These dots must be evenly spaced or the effect will be unsatisfactory. Baste the wadding to the fabric for the arms and back, taking the tacking stitches diagonally across the fabric, from corner to corner. Shave off a thickness of wadding around all edges so that it is thinner at the gluing lines. Beginning with the centre line of dots on the back piece and using a darker-coloured sewing thread, work horizontally in a zigzag pattern. Bring the needle through from the back of the fabric and across to the first dot. Pull the thread tight enough to form a slight swelling but not so tight that the fabric puckers. Secure with a small backstitch through the dot. Continue in this way until all the dots are joined (see Fig. 6). Turn under and tack down the seam allowances. Stitch the arms in the same way but do not turn under the allowance at the top outside edge.

6. Place the back piece in position and make sure that it will fit, adjusting the turning allowance if necessary. Use fabric glue and dress-making pins to hold the back in position. When glued firmly, smooth the fabric piece forward over the roll and glue and pin it in place where the seat joins the sofa-back. Cover the arms in the same way. Do not turn under the allowances on the outer arm edges above the "nick" marked. Catch-stitch the turned under edges, below the nick, to the edge of the arm front and fasten off. Run small gathering stitches along the arm roll edge, draw them up to form a rosette. Trim off any excess fabric before pressing in the upholstery pin. Catch stitch the fabric on the mitred corners together and fasten off.

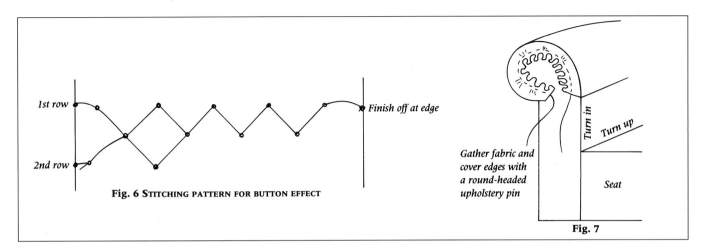

1st row *Finish off at edge*

2nd row

Fig. 6 STITCHING PATTERN FOR BUTTON EFFECT

Turn in *Turn up*

Gather fabric and cover edges with a round-headed upholstery pin

Seat

Fig. 7

7. Cut out the cushion cover pieces in fabric and wadding. Check the balsa cushion pieces for fit against the upholstered sofa, sanding off the excess if necessary. Glue the piece of wadding on the top of the cushion piece. Glue the back allowance of the fabric piece to the back of the balsa cushion, smoothing the fabric forwards over the wadding and gluing it in position under the front edge. Allow the glue to dry. Bend over the side edges, smoothing the fullness of the corners neatly and evenly around and under. Glue in place.

8. If you do not want to make a buttoned version, baste the wadding to the fabric and proceed as above. Remove all tacking stitches when the fabric pieces are glued in place.

9. Glue the squares of hard wood to the corners of the sofa to form feet.

Footstool

You Will Need
~

- 3mm (⅛in) wood, 38 × 25mm (1½ × 1in)
- 5mm (³⁄₁₆in) balsa wood, 22 × 35mm (⅞ × 1⅜in)
- Tapestry, petit point or suitable fabric to cover, 51 × 38mm (2 × 1½in)
- Thin wadding, 45 × 31mm (1¾ × 1¼in)
- Narrow trim (rickrack, cord or embossed paper), 127mm (5in)
- 4 tiny, round-headed, brass- or copper-finish upholstery pins, with 3mm (⅛in) heads for feet
- Fine sandpaper
- Wood glue
- Strong, non-staining fabric glue

1. Cut the base shape in wood and the smaller balsa wood shape. Soften the edges and corners of the balsa piece to make a cushion shape. Glue this to the wooden base.

2. Cut the wadding shape and glue it to the balsa wood. Glue the shorter sides, stroking the wadding outwards and down to achieve a smooth, taut surface. When it is firmly glued, stick down the longer sides. Use sharp scissors to snip away any excess so that the wadding does not overlap the base edges.

3. Cut the fabric pattern. First stick down the shorter sides, bringing the fabric flush with the edge of the base wood. When the glue is dry, smooth the fabric across from the longer edge and press it flush with the side of the base wood. Do not overlap the fabric under the base (see Fig. 5). Trim away any excess so that it is flush with the base.

4. Glue trim around the base edge.

5. Press pins into the bottom of the base as indicated on Fig. 1. If the shanks are too long, trim them with wire cutters or pliers and add a dab of wood glue to the shank before pushing them home. You may need a spiral drill to make the pin holes. If you do not have one, heat a needle and burn holes; this will stop the wood splitting.

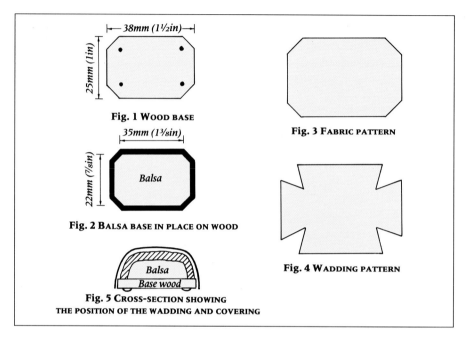

Fig. 1 WOOD BASE

Fig. 2 BALSA BASE IN PLACE ON WOOD

Fig. 3 FABRIC PATTERN

Fig. 4 WADDING PATTERN

Fig. 5 CROSS-SECTION SHOWING THE POSITION OF THE WADDING AND COVERING